T0288768

Decadence: A Very Short Introduction

VERY SHORT INTRODUCTIONS are for anyone wanting a stimulating and accessible way into a new subject. They are written by experts, and have been translated into more than 45 different languages.

The series began in 1995, and now covers a wide variety of topics in every discipline. The VSI library now contains over 500 volumes—a Very Short Introduction to everything from Psychology and Philosophy of Science to American History and Relativity—and continues to grow in every subject area.

Very Short Introductions available now:

ACCOUNTING Christopher Nobes
ADOLESCENCE Peter K. Smith
ADVERTISING Winston Fletcher
AFRICAN AMERICAN RELIGION Eddie S. Glaude Jr
AFRICAN HISTORY John Parker and Richard Rathbone
AFRICAN RELIGIONS Jacob K. Olupona
AGEING Nancy A. Pachana
AGNOSTICISM Robin Le Poidevin
AGRICULTURE Paul Brassley and Richard Soffe
ALEXANDER THE GREAT Hugh Bowden
ALGEBRA Peter M. Higgins
AMERICAN HISTORY Paul S. Boyer
AMERICAN IMMIGRATION David A. Gerber
AMERICAN LEGAL HISTORY G. Edward White
AMERICAN NAVAL HISTORY Craig L. Symonds
AMERICAN POLITICAL HISTORY Donald Critchlow
AMERICAN POLITICAL PARTIES AND ELECTIONS L. Sandy Maisel
AMERICAN POLITICS Richard M. Valelly
THE AMERICAN PRESIDENCY Charles O. Jones
THE AMERICAN REVOLUTION Robert J. Allison
AMERICAN SLAVERY Heather Andrea Williams
THE AMERICAN WEST Stephen Aron
AMERICAN WOMEN'S HISTORY Susan Ware
ANAESTHESIA Aidan O'Donnell
ANALYTIC PHILOSOPHY Michael Beaney
ANARCHISM Colin Ward
ANCIENT ASSYRIA Karen Radner
ANCIENT EGYPT Ian Shaw
ANCIENT EGYPTIAN ART AND ARCHITECTURE Christina Riggs
ANCIENT GREECE Paul Cartledge
THE ANCIENT NEAR EAST Amanda H. Podany
ANCIENT PHILOSOPHY Julia Annas
ANCIENT WARFARE Harry Sidebottom
ANGELS David Albert Jones
ANGLICANISM Mark Chapman
THE ANGLO-SAXON AGE John Blair
ANIMAL BEHAVIOUR Tristram D. Wyatt
THE ANIMAL KINGDOM Peter Holland
ANIMAL RIGHTS David DeGrazia
THE ANTARCTIC Klaus Dodds
ANTISEMITISM Steven Beller
ANXIETY Daniel Freeman and Jason Freeman
THE APOCRYPHAL GOSPELS Paul Foster
ARCHAEOLOGY Paul Bahn
ARCHITECTURE Andrew Ballantyne
ARISTOCRACY William Doyle
ARISTOTLE Jonathan Barnes

ART HISTORY Dana Arnold
ART THEORY Cynthia Freeland
ASIAN AMERICAN HISTORY Madeline Y. Hsu
ASTROBIOLOGY David C. Catling
ASTROPHYSICS James Binney
ATHEISM Julian Baggini
THE ATMOSPHERE Paul I. Palmer
AUGUSTINE Henry Chadwick
AUSTRALIA Kenneth Morgan
AUTISM Uta Frith
THE AVANT GARDE David Cottington
THE AZTECS Davíd Carrasco
BABYLONIA Trevor Bryce
BACTERIA Sebastian G. B. Amyes
BANKING John Goddard and John O. S. Wilson
BARTHES Jonathan Culler
THE BEATS David Sterritt
BEAUTY Roger Scruton
BEHAVIOURAL ECONOMICS Michelle Baddeley
BESTSELLERS John Sutherland
THE BIBLE John Riches
BIBLICAL ARCHAEOLOGY Eric H. Cline
BIG DATA Dawn E. Holmes
BIOGRAPHY Hermione Lee
BLACK HOLES Katherine Blundell
BLOOD Chris Cooper
THE BLUES Elijah Wald
THE BODY Chris Shilling
THE BOOK OF MORMON Terryl Givens
BORDERS Alexander C. Diener and Joshua Hagen
THE BRAIN Michael O'Shea
BRANDING Robert Jones
THE BRICS Andrew F. Cooper
THE BRITISH CONSTITUTION Martin Loughlin
THE BRITISH EMPIRE Ashley Jackson
BRITISH POLITICS Anthony Wright
BUDDHA Michael Carrithers
BUDDHISM Damien Keown
BUDDHIST ETHICS Damien Keown
BYZANTIUM Peter Sarris
CALVINISM Jon Balserak
CANCER Nicholas James
CAPITALISM James Fulcher
CATHOLICISM Gerald O'Collins
CAUSATION Stephen Mumford and Rani Lill Anjum
THE CELL Terence Allen and Graham Cowling
THE CELTS Barry Cunliffe
CHAOS Leonard Smith
CHEMISTRY Peter Atkins
CHILD PSYCHOLOGY Usha Goswami
CHILDREN'S LITERATURE Kimberley Reynolds
CHINESE LITERATURE Sabina Knight
CHOICE THEORY Michael Allingham
CHRISTIAN ART Beth Williamson
CHRISTIAN ETHICS D. Stephen Long
CHRISTIANITY Linda Woodhead
CIRCADIAN RHYTHMS Russell Foster and Leon Kreitzman
CITIZENSHIP Richard Bellamy
CIVIL ENGINEERING David Muir Wood
CLASSICAL LITERATURE William Allan
CLASSICAL MYTHOLOGY Helen Morales
CLASSICS Mary Beard and John Henderson
CLAUSEWITZ Michael Howard
CLIMATE Mark Maslin
CLIMATE CHANGE Mark Maslin
CLINICAL PSYCHOLOGY Susan Llewelyn and Katie Aafjes-van Doorn
COGNITIVE NEUROSCIENCE Richard Passingham
THE COLD WAR Robert McMahon
COLONIAL AMERICA Alan Taylor
COLONIAL LATIN AMERICAN LITERATURE Rolena Adorno
COMBINATORICS Robin Wilson
COMEDY Matthew Bevis
COMMUNISM Leslie Holmes
COMPLEXITY John H. Holland
THE COMPUTER Darrel Ince
COMPUTER SCIENCE Subrata Dasgupta
CONFUCIANISM Daniel K. Gardner
THE CONQUISTADORS Matthew Restall and Felipe Fernández-Armesto
CONSCIENCE Paul Strohm
CONSCIOUSNESS Susan Blackmore

CONTEMPORARY ART
Julian Stallabrass
CONTEMPORARY FICTION
Robert Eaglestone
CONTINENTAL PHILOSOPHY
Simon Critchley
COPERNICUS Owen Gingerich
CORAL REEFS Charles Sheppard
CORPORATE SOCIAL
RESPONSIBILITY
Jeremy Moon
CORRUPTION Leslie Holmes
COSMOLOGY Peter Coles
CRIME FICTION Richard Bradford
CRIMINAL JUSTICE Julian V. Roberts
CRITICAL THEORY
Stephen Eric Bronner
THE CRUSADES Christopher Tyerman
CRYPTOGRAPHY Fred Piper and
Sean Murphy
CRYSTALLOGRAPHY A. M. Glazer
THE CULTURAL REVOLUTION
Richard Curt Kraus
DADA AND SURREALISM
David Hopkins
DANTE Peter Hainsworth and
David Robey
DARWIN Jonathan Howard
THE DEAD SEA SCROLLS
Timothy H. Lim
DECOLONIZATION Dane Kennedy
DEMOCRACY Bernard Crick
DEPRESSION Jan Scott and
Mary Jane Tacchi
DERRIDA Simon Glendinning
DESCARTES Tom Sorell
DESERTS Nick Middleton
DESIGN John Heskett
DEVELOPMENTAL BIOLOGY
Lewis Wolpert
THE DEVIL Darren Oldridge
DIASPORA Kevin Kenny
DICTIONARIES Lynda Mugglestone
DINOSAURS David Norman
DIPLOMACY Joseph M. Siracusa
DOCUMENTARY FILM
Patricia Aufderheide
DREAMING J. Allan Hobson
DRUGS Les Iversen
DRUIDS Barry Cunliffe
EARLY MUSIC Thomas Forrest Kelly
THE EARTH Martin Redfern
EARTH SYSTEM SCIENCE
Tim Lenton
ECONOMICS Partha Dasgupta
EDUCATION Gary Thomas
EGYPTIAN MYTH Geraldine Pinch
EIGHTEENTH-CENTURY BRITAIN
Paul Langford
THE ELEMENTS Philip Ball
EMOTION Dylan Evans
EMPIRE Stephen Howe
ENGELS Terrell Carver
ENGINEERING David Blockley
ENGLISH LITERATURE Jonathan Bate
THE ENLIGHTENMENT
John Robertson
ENTREPRENEURSHIP
Paul Westhead and Mike Wright
ENVIRONMENTAL ECONOMICS
Stephen Smith
ENVIRONMENTAL LAW
Elizabeth Fisher
ENVIRONMENTAL POLITICS
Andrew Dobson
EPICUREANISM Catherine Wilson
EPIDEMIOLOGY Rodolfo Saracci
ETHICS Simon Blackburn
ETHNOMUSICOLOGY Timothy Rice
THE ETRUSCANS Christopher Smith
EUGENICS Philippa Levine
THE EUROPEAN UNION
John Pinder and Simon Usherwood
EUROPEAN UNION LAW
Anthony Arnull
EVOLUTION Brian and
Deborah Charlesworth
EXISTENTIALISM Thomas Flynn
EXPLORATION Stewart A. Weaver
THE EYE Michael Land
FAMILY LAW Jonathan Herring
FASCISM Kevin Passmore
FASHION Rebecca Arnold
FEMINISM Margaret Walters
FILM Michael Wood
FILM MUSIC Kathryn Kalinak
THE FIRST WORLD WAR
Michael Howard
FOLK MUSIC Mark Slobin
FOOD John Krebs

FORENSIC PSYCHOLOGY David Canter
FORENSIC SCIENCE Jim Fraser
FORESTS Jaboury Ghazoul
FOSSILS Keith Thomson
FOUCAULT Gary Gutting
THE FOUNDING FATHERS R. B. Bernstein
FRACTALS Kenneth Falconer
FREE SPEECH Nigel Warburton
FREE WILL Thomas Pink
FREEMASONRY Andreas Önnerfors
FRENCH LITERATURE John D. Lyons
THE FRENCH REVOLUTION William Doyle
FREUD Anthony Storr
FUNDAMENTALISM Malise Ruthven
FUNGI Nicholas P. Money
THE FUTURE Jennifer M. Gidley
GALAXIES John Gribbin
GALILEO Stillman Drake
GAME THEORY Ken Binmore
GANDHI Bhikhu Parekh
GENES Jonathan Slack
GENIUS Andrew Robinson
GEOGRAPHY John Matthews and David Herbert
GEOPOLITICS Klaus Dodds
GERMAN LITERATURE Nicholas Boyle
GERMAN PHILOSOPHY Andrew Bowie
GLOBAL CATASTROPHES Bill McGuire
GLOBAL ECONOMIC HISTORY Robert C. Allen
GLOBALIZATION Manfred Steger
GOD John Bowker
GOETHE Ritchie Robertson
THE GOTHIC Nick Groom
GOVERNANCE Mark Bevir
GRAVITY Timothy Clifton
THE GREAT DEPRESSION AND THE NEW DEAL Eric Rauchway
HABERMAS James Gordon Finlayson
THE HABSBURG EMPIRE Martyn Rady
HAPPINESS Daniel M. Haybron
THE HARLEM RENAISSANCE Cheryl A. Wall
THE HEBREW BIBLE AS LITERATURE Tod Linafelt
HEGEL Peter Singer
HEIDEGGER Michael Inwood
HEREDITY John Waller
HERMENEUTICS Jens Zimmermann
HERODOTUS Jennifer T. Roberts
HIEROGLYPHS Penelope Wilson
HINDUISM Kim Knott
HISTORY John H. Arnold
THE HISTORY OF ASTRONOMY Michael Hoskin
THE HISTORY OF CHEMISTRY William H. Brock
THE HISTORY OF CINEMA Geoffrey Nowell-Smith
THE HISTORY OF LIFE Michael Benton
THE HISTORY OF MATHEMATICS Jacqueline Stedall
THE HISTORY OF MEDICINE William Bynum
THE HISTORY OF TIME Leofranc Holford-Strevens
HIV AND AIDS Alan Whiteside
HOBBES Richard Tuck
HOLLYWOOD Peter Decherney
HOME Michael Allen Fox
HORMONES Martin Luck
HUMAN ANATOMY Leslie Klenerman
HUMAN EVOLUTION Bernard Wood
HUMAN RIGHTS Andrew Clapham
HUMANISM Stephen Law
HUME A. J. Ayer
HUMOUR Noël Carroll
THE ICE AGE Jamie Woodward
IDEOLOGY Michael Freeden
THE IMMUNE SYSTEM Paul Klenerman
INDIAN CINEMA Ashish Rajadhyaksha
INDIAN PHILOSOPHY Sue Hamilton
THE INDUSTRIAL REVOLUTION Robert C. Allen
INFECTIOUS DISEASE Marta L. Wayne and Benjamin M. Bolker
INFINITY Ian Stewart
INFORMATION Luciano Floridi
INNOVATION Mark Dodgson and David Gann
INTELLIGENCE Ian J. Deary

INTELLECTUAL PROPERTY Siva Vaidhyanathan
INTERNATIONAL LAW Vaughan Lowe
INTERNATIONAL MIGRATION Khalid Koser
INTERNATIONAL RELATIONS Paul Wilkinson
INTERNATIONAL SECURITY Christopher S. Browning
IRAN Ali M. Ansari
ISLAM Malise Ruthven
ISLAMIC HISTORY Adam Silverstein
ISOTOPES Rob Ellam
ITALIAN LITERATURE Peter Hainsworth and David Robey
JESUS Richard Bauckham
JEWISH HISTORY David N. Myers
JOURNALISM Ian Hargreaves
JUDAISM Norman Solomon
JUNG Anthony Stevens
KABBALAH Joseph Dan
KAFKA Ritchie Robertson
KANT Roger Scruton
KEYNES Robert Skidelsky
KIERKEGAARD Patrick Gardiner
KNOWLEDGE Jennifer Nagel
THE KORAN Michael Cook
LANDSCAPE ARCHITECTURE Ian H. Thompson
LANDSCAPES AND GEOMORPHOLOGY Andrew Goudie and Heather Viles
LANGUAGES Stephen R. Anderson
LATE ANTIQUITY Gillian Clark
LAW Raymond Wacks
THE LAWS OF THERMODYNAMICS Peter Atkins
LEADERSHIP Keith Grint
LEARNING Mark Haselgrove
LEIBNIZ Maria Rosa Antognazza
LIBERALISM Michael Freeden
LIGHT Ian Walmsley
LINCOLN Allen C. Guelzo
LINGUISTICS Peter Matthews
LITERARY THEORY Jonathan Culler
LOCKE John Dunn
LOGIC Graham Priest
LOVE Ronald de Sousa
MACHIAVELLI Quentin Skinner
MADNESS Andrew Scull
MAGIC Owen Davies
MAGNA CARTA Nicholas Vincent
MAGNETISM Stephen Blundell
MALTHUS Donald Winch
MAMMALS T. S. Kemp
MANAGEMENT John Hendry
MAO Delia Davin
MARINE BIOLOGY Philip V. Mladenov
THE MARQUIS DE SADE John Phillips
MARTIN LUTHER Scott H. Hendrix
MARTYRDOM Jolyon Mitchell
MARX Peter Singer
MATERIALS Christopher Hall
MATHEMATICS Timothy Gowers
THE MEANING OF LIFE Terry Eagleton
MEASUREMENT David Hand
MEDICAL ETHICS Tony Hope
MEDICAL LAW Charles Foster
MEDIEVAL BRITAIN John Gillingham and Ralph A. Griffiths
MEDIEVAL LITERATURE Elaine Treharne
MEDIEVAL PHILOSOPHY John Marenbon
MEMORY Jonathan K. Foster
METAPHYSICS Stephen Mumford
THE MEXICAN REVOLUTION Alan Knight
MICHAEL FARADAY Frank A. J. L. James
MICROBIOLOGY Nicholas P. Money
MICROECONOMICS Avinash Dixit
MICROSCOPY Terence Allen
THE MIDDLE AGES Miri Rubin
MILITARY JUSTICE Eugene R. Fidell
MILITARY STRATEGY Antulio J. Echevarria II
MINERALS David Vaughan
MIRACLES Yujin Nagasawa
MODERN ART David Cottington
MODERN CHINA Rana Mitter
MODERN DRAMA Kirsten E. Shepherd-Barr
MODERN FRANCE Vanessa R. Schwartz
MODERN INDIA Craig Jeffrey
MODERN IRELAND Senia Pašeta

MODERN ITALY Anna Cento Bull
MODERN JAPAN Christopher Goto-Jones
MODERN LATIN AMERICAN LITERATURE Roberto González Echevarría
MODERN WAR Richard English
MODERNISM Christopher Butler
MOLECULAR BIOLOGY Aysha Divan and Janice A. Royds
MOLECULES Philip Ball
THE MONGOLS Morris Rossabi
MOONS David A. Rothery
MORMONISM Richard Lyman Bushman
MOUNTAINS Martin F. Price
MUHAMMAD Jonathan A. C. Brown
MULTICULTURALISM Ali Rattansi
MULTILINGUALISM John C. Maher
MUSIC Nicholas Cook
MYTH Robert A. Segal
THE NAPOLEONIC WARS Mike Rapport
NATIONALISM Steven Grosby
NATIVE AMERICAN LITERATURE Sean Teuton
NAVIGATION Jim Bennett
NELSON MANDELA Elleke Boehmer
NEOLIBERALISM Manfred Steger and Ravi Roy
NETWORKS Guido Caldarelli and Michele Catanzaro
THE NEW TESTAMENT Luke Timothy Johnson
THE NEW TESTAMENT AS LITERATURE Kyle Keefer
NEWTON Robert Iliffe
NIETZSCHE Michael Tanner
NINETEENTH-CENTURY BRITAIN Christopher Harvie and H. C. G. Matthew
THE NORMAN CONQUEST George Garnett
NORTH AMERICAN INDIANS Theda Perdue and Michael D. Green
NORTHERN IRELAND Marc Mulholland
NOTHING Frank Close
NUCLEAR PHYSICS Frank Close
NUCLEAR POWER Maxwell Irvine
NUCLEAR WEAPONS Joseph M. Siracusa
NUMBERS Peter M. Higgins
NUTRITION David A. Bender
OBJECTIVITY Stephen Gaukroger
OCEANS Dorrik Stow
THE OLD TESTAMENT Michael D. Coogan
THE ORCHESTRA D. Kern Holoman
ORGANIC CHEMISTRY Graham Patrick
ORGANIZATIONS Mary Jo Hatch
PAGANISM Owen Davies
PAIN Rob Boddice
THE PALESTINIAN-ISRAELI CONFLICT Martin Bunton
PANDEMICS Christian W. McMillen
PARTICLE PHYSICS Frank Close
PAUL E. P. Sanders
PEACE Oliver P. Richmond
PENTECOSTALISM William K. Kay
PERCEPTION Brian Rogers
THE PERIODIC TABLE Eric R. Scerri
PHILOSOPHY Edward Craig
PHILOSOPHY IN THE ISLAMIC WORLD Peter Adamson
PHILOSOPHY OF LAW Raymond Wacks
PHILOSOPHY OF SCIENCE Samir Okasha
PHOTOGRAPHY Steve Edwards
PHYSICAL CHEMISTRY Peter Atkins
PILGRIMAGE Ian Reader
PLAGUE Paul Slack
PLANETS David A. Rothery
PLANTS Timothy Walker
PLATE TECTONICS Peter Molnar
PLATO Julia Annas
POLITICAL PHILOSOPHY David Miller
POLITICS Kenneth Minogue
POPULISM Cas Mudde and Cristóbal Rovira Kaltwasser
POSTCOLONIALISM Robert Young
POSTMODERNISM Christopher Butler
POSTSTRUCTURALISM Catherine Belsey
PREHISTORY Chris Gosden
PRESOCRATIC PHILOSOPHY Catherine Osborne

PRIVACY Raymond Wacks
PROBABILITY John Haigh
PROGRESSIVISM Walter Nugent
PROJECTS Andrew Davies
PROTESTANTISM Mark A. Noll
PSYCHIATRY Tom Burns
PSYCHOANALYSIS Daniel Pick
PSYCHOLOGY Gillian Butler and Freda McManus
PSYCHOTHERAPY Tom Burns and Eva Burns-Lundgren
PUBLIC ADMINISTRATION Stella Z. Theodoulou and Ravi K. Roy
PUBLIC HEALTH Virginia Berridge
PURITANISM Francis J. Bremer
THE QUAKERS Pink Dandelion
QUANTUM THEORY John Polkinghorne
RACISM Ali Rattansi
RADIOACTIVITY Claudio Tuniz
RASTAFARI Ennis B. Edmonds
THE REAGAN REVOLUTION Gil Troy
REALITY Jan Westerhoff
THE REFORMATION Peter Marshall
RELATIVITY Russell Stannard
RELIGION IN AMERICA Timothy Beal
THE RENAISSANCE Jerry Brotton
RENAISSANCE ART Geraldine A. Johnson
REVOLUTIONS Jack A. Goldstone
RHETORIC Richard Toye
RISK Baruch Fischhoff and John Kadvany
RITUAL Barry Stephenson
RIVERS Nick Middleton
ROBOTICS Alan Winfield
ROCKS Jan Zalasiewicz
ROMAN BRITAIN Peter Salway
THE ROMAN EMPIRE Christopher Kelly
THE ROMAN REPUBLIC David M. Gwynn
ROMANTICISM Michael Ferber
ROUSSEAU Robert Wokler
RUSSELL A. C. Grayling
RUSSIAN HISTORY Geoffrey Hosking
RUSSIAN LITERATURE Catriona Kelly
THE RUSSIAN REVOLUTION S. A. Smith
SAVANNAS Peter A. Furley
SCHIZOPHRENIA Chris Frith and Eve Johnstone
SCHOPENHAUER Christopher Janaway
SCIENCE AND RELIGION Thomas Dixon
SCIENCE FICTION David Seed
THE SCIENTIFIC REVOLUTION Lawrence M. Principe
SCOTLAND Rab Houston
SEXUALITY Véronique Mottier
SHAKESPEARE'S COMEDIES Bart van Es
SHAKESPEARE'S SONNETS AND POEMS Jonathan F. S. Post
SHAKESPEARE'S TRAGEDIES Stanley Wells
SIKHISM Eleanor Nesbitt
THE SILK ROAD James A. Millward
SLANG Jonathon Green
SLEEP Steven W. Lockley and Russell G. Foster
SOCIAL AND CULTURAL ANTHROPOLOGY John Monaghan and Peter Just
SOCIAL PSYCHOLOGY Richard J. Crisp
SOCIAL WORK Sally Holland and Jonathan Scourfield
SOCIALISM Michael Newman
SOCIOLINGUISTICS John Edwards
SOCIOLOGY Steve Bruce
SOCRATES C. C. W. Taylor
SOUND Mike Goldsmith
THE SOVIET UNION Stephen Lovell
THE SPANISH CIVIL WAR Helen Graham
SPANISH LITERATURE Jo Labanyi
SPINOZA Roger Scruton
SPIRITUALITY Philip Sheldrake
SPORT Mike Cronin
STARS Andrew King
STATISTICS David J. Hand
STEM CELLS Jonathan Slack
STRUCTURAL ENGINEERING David Blockley
STUART BRITAIN John Morrill
SUPERCONDUCTIVITY Stephen Blundell
SYMMETRY Ian Stewart
TAXATION Stephen Smith
TEETH Peter S. Ungar

TELESCOPES Geoff Cottrell
TERRORISM Charles Townshend
THEATRE Marvin Carlson
THEOLOGY David F. Ford
THINKING AND REASONING
Jonathan St B. T. Evans
THOMAS AQUINAS Fergus Kerr
THOUGHT Tim Bayne
TIBETAN BUDDHISM
Matthew T. Kapstein
TOCQUEVILLE Harvey C. Mansfield
TRAGEDY Adrian Poole
TRANSLATION Matthew Reynolds
THE TROJAN WAR Eric H. Cline
TRUST Katherine Hawley
THE TUDORS John Guy
TWENTIETH-CENTURY BRITAIN
Kenneth O. Morgan
THE UNITED NATIONS
Jussi M. Hanhimäki
THE U.S. CONGRESS
Donald A. Ritchie
THE U.S. SUPREME COURT
Linda Greenhouse
UTILITARIANISM
Katarzyna de Lazari-Radek and
Peter Singer
UTOPIANISM Lyman Tower Sargent
THE VIKINGS Julian Richards
VIRUSES Dorothy H. Crawford
VOLTAIRE Nicholas Cronk
WAR AND TECHNOLOGY
Alex Roland
WATER John Finney
WEATHER Storm Dunlop
THE WELFARE STATE David Garland
WILLIAM SHAKESPEARE
Stanley Wells
WITCHCRAFT Malcolm Gaskill
WITTGENSTEIN A. C. Grayling
WORK Stephen Fineman
WORLD MUSIC Philip Bohlman
THE WORLD TRADE
ORGANIZATION Amrita Narlikar
WORLD WAR II Gerhard L. Weinberg
WRITING AND SCRIPT
Andrew Robinson
ZIONISM Michael Stanislawski

Available soon:

THE UNIVERSITY David Palfreyman
and Paul Temple
VETERINARY SCIENCE
James Yeates
MONASTICISM Stephen J. Davis
THE ENGLISH LANGUAGE
Simon Horobin
FAIRY TALES Marina Warner

For more information visit our website

www.oup.com/vsi/

David Weir

DECADENCE

A Very Short Introduction

OXFORD
UNIVERSITY PRESS

OXFORD
UNIVERSITY PRESS

Oxford University Press is a department of the University of Oxford. It furthers the University's objective of excellence in research, scholarship, and education by publishing worldwide. Oxford is a registered trademark of Oxford University Press in the UK and certain other countries.

Published in the United States of America by Oxford University Press
198 Madison Avenue, New York, NY 10016, United States of America.

© Oxford University Press 2018

All rights reserved. No part of this publication may be reproduced, stored in a retrieval system, or transmitted, in any form or by any means, without the prior permission in writing of Oxford University Press, or as expressly permitted by law, by license, or under terms agreed with the appropriate reproduction rights organization. Inquiries concerning reproduction outside the scope of the above should be sent to the Rights Department, Oxford University Press, at the address above.

You must not circulate this work in any other form
and you must impose this same condition on any acquirer.

Library of Congress Cataloging-in-Publication Data
Names: Weir, David, 1947 April 20- author.
Title: Decadence : a very short introduction / David Weir.
Description: Oxford ; New York : Oxford University Press, [2018] | Includes bibliographical references and index.
Identifiers: LCCN 2017036015 (print) | LCCN 2017045584 (ebook) | ISBN 9780190610258 (online component) | ISBN 9780190610234 (updf) | ISBN 9780190610241 (epub) | ISBN 9780190610227 (pbk. : alk. paper)
Subjects: LCSH: Degeneration—Social aspects—History. | Moral conditions—History. | Intellectual life—History. | Civilization—History.
Classification: LCC HM892 (ebook) | LCC HM892 .W45 2018 (print) | DDC 303.48—dc23
LC record available at https://lccn.loc.gov/2017036015

Links to third party websites are provided by Oxford in good faith and for information only. Oxford disclaims any responsibility for the materials contained in any third party website referenced in this work.

Printed by Integrated Books International, United States of America

La chair est triste, hélas! et j'ai lu tous les livres.
(The flesh is sad, alas! and I have read all the books.)

—Stéphane Mallarmé, "Brise Marine"

In memory of David Geoffrey Weir

Contents

List of illustrations

Acknowledgments

A very short introduction to decadence? How is that possible? Nancy Toff, that's how. One of the few real editors I have ever had, Nancy guided this project from beginning to end with grace, intelligence, and humor. I am grateful to her and her two able assistants at Oxford University Press, Elda Granada and Elizabeth Vaziri, for being both personable and professional.

I am also grateful to numerous students at the Cooper Union for the Advancement of Science and Art in New York City for being so receptive to decadence over the years. One of them suggested I write this book, so I have to offer her special thanks by mentioning her special name: so, thank you, Theresa Zeitz-Lindamood.

This is my third book on decadence, so for the third time I thank my wife, Camille—for living up to her nineteenth-century name. One could not ask for a better partner in decline.

Introduction

Decadence is a simple word but a complicated concept: the Latin verb *decadēre* means "to decay," formed by the root verb *cadēre* "to fall" plus the prefix *de-* "down." The Latin origins of the word are of interest not only to etymologists but also to historians: after all, Latin was the language of ancient Rome, and everyone knows that Rome fell, down, into a state of decay. The fall of Rome furnishes us with the first of several seemingly simple interpretations of the word decadence: historical decline. The decline and fall of the Roman Empire also points to a second shading of the concept: social decay. The political corruption and excessive hedonism of any number of Roman emperors—Caligula, Nero, Elagabalus, to name a few—earned them the epithet *decadent*, first in the work of professional historians and, later, more broadly, in the popular imagination. Crucially, the personal depravity of a Caligula or a Nero is regarded as an index to the broader degeneration of society at large.

Moreover, the historical decline and social decay of ancient Rome was also reflected in the literature of the age, which leads to a third important sense of decadence: aesthetic inferiority. The art produced in periods of historical decline is regarded as inferior to the work of artists and writers of an earlier age, when the empire or the nation is at the height of its political power and economic influence. Virgil, who wrote during the reign of Augustus Caesar

(r. 27 BCE – 14 CE), is the great poet of empire, but Ausonius, who wrote during the reign of Valentinian (r. 364–375 CE) after Rome had entered the period of its long decline, is a minor writer of the Decadence, not so much a poet as a poetaster, an inferior imitator of the patterns of the past. The historical, social, and aesthetic dimensions of decadence are all covered, but they are also questioned and qualified.

Consider, for example, "the decadence of Rome." Obviously, the Roman Empire no longer exists. But more than nine hundred million people today speak a language that developed from one of the vernacular dialects of Latin spoken two thousand years ago somewhere in the Roman Empire. French and Spanish, for example, are called Romance languages because they evolved from the language spoken by the Romans who colonized the ancient imperial provinces of Gaul (modern France) and Hispania (modern Spain). Another example of the continuing relevance of ancient Rome is the system of laws used to administer the republic and, later, the empire. A modified version of that system remains in use today, mostly in Europe but also in parts of Asia and Africa that were once under Roman control.

In the United States, the Founding Fathers may have relied more on British common law than on Roman law in crafting the American legal system, but they looked to the Roman Republic as a model of representative government, naming part of that government, the Senate, after its Roman prototype, *Senatus*. The linguistic, legal, and political resonance of ancient Rome is matched by its ongoing religious influence. The deathbed conversion of Emperor Constantine (r. 306–337 CE) aided the spread of Christianity throughout the empire, assuring the establishment of the Holy Roman Catholic and Apostolic Church. Add to all this the achievements of Roman architecture and engineering (the roads, the aqueducts, the sewers) that have had a lasting influence on the built environment of so many cities, and the question quite reasonably arises: "What kind of decadence is this, really?"

The question arises because decay, it turns out, is oddly generative: the historical decline of Rome ultimately seems less like decadence and more like progress because of the many social and cultural developments that ensued in the wake of both the Roman Republic and the Roman Empire. Rome not only remains the paradigm of decadence, it also provides the pattern for the inevitable linkage of decline and renewal. But this pattern becomes a paradox in the modern era: historical decline and renewal, social decay and regeneration, artistic decadence and avant-gardism appear increasingly interrelated. In fact, modernity itself seems to call for a decadent response of one kind or another, so much so that decadence today may perhaps best be understood as the aesthetic expression of a conflicted attitude toward modernity. Decadence and modernity are not precisely contemporary with one another, but if we think of modernity as the vast complex of social, political, and technological transformations that emerged in the early nineteenth century, decadence—or the perception thereof—was not far behind.

The conflicted sense of modernity that decadence describes arises first and most clearly in nineteenth-century France. The English word "decadence" derives from French *décadence*, an etymological fact that might serve as a capsule description of a much broader cultural development: in the modern era, just about every manifestation of decadence owes its origins, either directly or indirectly, to a loosely affiliated group of artists and writers who lived and worked in Paris. French decadence should really be called "Parisian decadence" because decadence is deeply urbanist. The philosopher Walter Benjamin famously termed Paris the "Capital of the Nineteenth Century" since for him the city illustrated, better than most, the social and demographic trends that constitute modernity: the mass migration of people from the country to the town, the growth of consumer culture, the advent of new technologies (in transportation, architecture, infrastructure), and many more developments that we take for granted today.

The proponents of modernity interpret its effects as progress, and indeed it is the case that most of the changes in the built environment that Louis-Napoléon contemplated and that Baron Hausmann executed in Paris during the Second Empire (1852–1870) improved the lives of its citizens (sanitation and transportation are two obvious areas of improvement). But not everyone experienced this new urban modernity as progress; those who didn't regarded progress itself as decadence. The accelerated rhythm of modernity, the up-tempo cadence of daily life, was, for some, de-cadence.

The one author who best expressed the conflicted attitude toward modernity in nineteenth century Paris was Charles Baudelaire (1821–1867). In an essay on Edgar Allan Poe, Baudelaire called progress "that great heresy of decline" and regarded it as nothing more than "an idiot's delight." What Haussmann called improvements Poe preferred to term "rectangular obscenities." The critic Théophile Gautier (1811–1872) ascribed that assessment of modernity to Baudelaire himself while also praising the poet for writing in "the decadent style, which is simply art that has reached the extreme point of maturity which marks the setting of ancient civilizations." In Gautier's formulation, then, the Paris of Baudelaire, the capital of nineteenth-century progress, is also the capital of an ancient civilization in decline. More important, the modern urban world, with all its temptations and contradictions, calls for a new kind of artistic response—a new kind of artist, really. Gautier saw Baudelaire as precisely the poet of modern life who possessed the new aesthetic sensibility necessary to capture the complexities of that life. No doubt he was able to do this because Baudelaire himself had described that sensibility in one of the most important documents of decadence: "The Painter of Modern Life" (1863).

Baudelaire's essay is ostensibly an appreciation of Constantin Guys (1802–1892), an illustrator whose sketches appeared in British and French newspapers. Guys is not named directly, referred to only as "Monsieur M. G." or "Monsieur G."—an indication, perhaps, that Baudelaire is more concerned with the nature of modern life and the problem of "painting" or representing it than he is with the work of a particular artist. The essay begins by describing the traditional aesthetic category of Beauty in an untraditional way: Beauty is really twofold, containing "an eternal, invariable element" and "a relative, circumstantial element." This second element is modernity, "the ephemeral, the fugitive, the contingent, the half of art whose other half is the eternal and immutable." This is not a very complicated idea of modernity—all Baudelaire is asking of art is that it reflect present reality—but it was revolutionary at the time. The kind of rapid technique required to capture contemporary scenes and events necessarily breaks with the careful, studied art of classicism, and the focus on the present breaks with the penchant for the past that we identify with romanticism. The kind of art Baudelaire has in mind, then, seems a lot like what we now call modernism.

But it isn't really, or isn't fully, because Baudelaire expresses a number of reservations about the pageant of modern life he sees all around him. The disaffection he feels is conveyed though the opposition of two important terms: "flâneur" and "dandy." The first term describes a man who lounges about the cafés or saunters down the boulevards, taking pleasure in observation alone. As a "painter of the passing moment," Monsieur G. has much in common with the flâneur because he takes interest in that moment but without participating in it: "The artist lives very little, if at all, in the world of morals or politics." That world is the domain of the dandy, who is not a "passionate spectator" like the flâneur, but someone who "aspires to insensitivity."

The dandy, in short, is blasé—"for reasons of policy and caste." The comment about caste becomes clear when Baudelaire explains that the dandy necessarily possesses an "aristocratic superiority of mind." By this point in the essay, it is clear that Baudelaire is really talking about himself as the painter—or the poet—of modern life, and that modern life is really a form of decadence, because "dandyism appears above all in periods of transition, when democracy is not yet all-powerful, and aristocracy is only just beginning to totter and fall." It follows that "dandyism is the last spark of heroism amid decadence." Both of the character types that Baudelaire describes—the flâneur and the dandy—are, like the decadent, creatures of modern urban society. Like the flâneur, the decadent observes but does not participate in modern life, possibly taking some pleasure in what he sees, but not much. Decadents are more like dandies, especially in their cultivation of aristocratic tastes and in their revulsion over the rise of democracy and the emergence of mass society.

Paris was not the only capital of the nineteenth century that produced a culture of decadence that celebrated some aspects of modernity but resisted others, but it was the first. Paris produced the first poet (Baudelaire) to be retrospectively described as decadent by the first critic of decadence (Gautier). Paris also boasts the first novelist of decadence in Joris-Karl Huysmans (1848–1907), whose novel *À Rebours* (1884) had enormous influence on the next generation of decadents (the title of the novel has been translated as *Against the Grain* and *Against Nature*). That generation was mostly British, so one can say that decadence in the nineteenth century "travels" from Paris to London, and it does so because so many Londoners of the time who were interested in literature and art traveled to Paris and brought decadence back home with them.

The best known of these London decadents is undoubtedly Oscar Wilde, whose distinction lies in combining the French decadent tradition exemplified by Huysmans with the British aesthetic tradition exemplified by Walter Pater (1839–1894), a classics professor who taught Wilde at Oxford University. The title character of Wilde's only novel, *The Picture of Dorian Gray* (1891), is both an aesthete and a hedonist, a lover of fine art and a connoisseur of opium. The novel also contains suggestions of male homosexuality that are so compelling that passages from *Dorian Gray* were read at Wilde's trials as evidence against him for committing the crime of "gross indecency." Wilde's conviction and imprisonment in 1895 had a profound and disturbing effect on what was by that time a decadent movement, and not just in England. American decadents in Boston, for example, were thoroughly shaken by what happened to Wilde and feared that the same thing might happen to the queer members of their own movement, since same-sex love was a criminal offense in the United States just as it was in Great Britain.

Paris and London are the cities most central to the development of decadence. But Paris and London are obviously not the only metropolitan centers where urban renovation, population migration, technological transformation, political reformation, and other markers of modernity occurred during the latter half of the nineteenth century. Vienna is another nineteenth-century capital of modernity that makes up part of the urban geography of decadence, and so is Berlin. But the political and social conditions most conducive to the culture of decadence do not coalesce in the case of Berlin until the twentieth century, during the period of the Weimar Republic (1919–1933). Decadence is hard to date, and not everyone would say that it extends so far into the twentieth century as the end of the Weimar era. A case can be made, however, that decadence reached its peak in the second decade of the Third Republic in France (the 1880s), in the last decade of Queen Victoria's reign in Great Britain (the 1890s), in the middle decade of Archduke Ferdinand's status as heir to the throne of Austria-Hungary (the early 1900s), and in the tumultuous decade of the Weimar Republic (the 1920s).

These decades of decadence are of course approximate—there are things to say about decadence before 1880 and after 1930—and during that fifty-year period decadence is not centered exclusively in Paris, London, Vienna, and Berlin. Boston decadence is contemporary with London decadence, just as Hollywood decadence matches (in more than one way) that of Berlin in the 1920s. As decadence travels from one city to another, its inherent artistic and social dimensions undergo a series of transformations. London decadence appears to integrate aesthetic style and personal behavior more so than Parisian decadence does. In Vienna, the identification of decadence with the diminishing aristocratic class begins to change and the "bourgeoisification" of decadence begins. By the time decadence reaches Weimar Berlin it is no longer the province or the practice of elites. Ultimately, this democratization of decadence results in its migration into popular culture. Indeed, decadence has enjoyed a considerable afterlife in that over-the-top culture known as camp, which the critic Susan Sontag helpfully clarified as an ability to discriminate between inferior art and deliberately inferior art—"the good taste of bad taste."

That definition of camp should not be taken as a definition of decadence, although the camp sensibility does demonstrate the conflicted attitude toward modernity that we have identified with decadence. Our initial attempt to define decadence was etymological and historical, and that effort remains meaningful. But decadence is more than decline, decay, and degeneration, whether artistic, historical, or social. We need to keep those meanings in mind, certainly, while also keeping in mind a number of nuances and implications. Think of decadence as an ornate, highly artificial object that resembles nothing in nature, represented on a slide projected through an old-fashioned magic lantern, seen through a series of colored filters, each color representing a different aspect of decadence. The object, in other words, takes on a different coloration depending on the filter. One filter darkens the object and makes decadence look like pessimism; another gives it a luscious hue that makes it look like hedonism; a mottled, greenish filter turns the object rotten, suggesting degeneration; still another imparts a lavender glow and connotes, somehow, "the love that dare not speak its name" (the phrase Lord Alfred Douglas, Oscar Wilde's lover, used to describe homosexuality). But whatever coloration decadence takes, it is typically the expression—the projection—of urban experience.

We should not expect to find every aspect of decadence in the same work at the same time. Truly representative, comprehensive examples of decadence are hard to find. But one poem comes closer than most: Paul Verlaine's sonnet "Langueur." The poem is presented in French because so much of it has no exact equivalent in English, starting with the title. Yes, "Langueur" means "languor" or "lassitude," but the sense of weary listlessness comes across better in the French word, which has the accent on the second syllable rather than the first so it can be lazily drawn out, matching sound to sense.

Likewise, a straightforward translation of the first line—"I am the Empire at the end of the decadence"—misses the limping rhythm of the French alexandrine, the twelve-syllable line divided into groups of three. The line was a staple of the clear, balanced prosody of French classicistic poets and dramatists like Racine

Verlaine's "Langueur"

Je suis l'Empire à la fin de la décadence,
Qui regarde passer les grands Barbares blancs
En composant des acrostiches indolents
D'un style d'or où la langueur du soleil danse.

L'âme seulette a mal au cœur d'un ennui dense.
Là-bas on dit qu'il est de longs combats sanglants.
Ô n'y pouvoir, étant si faible aux vœux si lents,
Ô n'y vouloir fleurir un peu cette existence!

Ô n'y vouloir, ô n'y pouvoir mourir un peu!
Ah! tout est bu! Bathylle, as-tu fini de rire?
Ah, tout est bu, tout est mangé! Plus rien à dire!

Seul, un poème un peu niais qu'on jette au feu,
Seul, un esclave un peu coureur qui vous néglige,
Seul, un ennui d'on ne sait quoi qui vous afflige!

Paul Verlaine (1884)

before Verlaine, following his romantic precursors, loosened up the line and made it more flexible and expressive. In fact, the first four lines of the poem are mostly about literary style during a decadent period. The poem opens by personifying the Roman Empire itself in the last days of decline, passively watching its own destruction by the giant barbarians from the north (*les grands Barbares blancs*) while composing "indolent acrostics in a golden style" (*des acrostiches indolents/D'un style d'or*). In an acrostic, the first letters of each line spell out a word or phrase, so the form is by definition highly artificial, as is the notion of a golden style, that is, a style that is needlessly ornate.

The setting for this lazy literary activity is most likely sunset, since the sun itself seems to have been affected by the mood of weariness (*la langueur du soleil*). Despite vague reports of a long, bloody battle (*de longs combats sanglants*), the speaker of the poem does not feel threatened at all—only bored: the lonely soul is heartsick with a feeling of ennui so intense, so "dense," that he has no energy for anything, not even, it seems, his own death. He wishes *not* to be able (*Ô n'y pouvoir*) to act on his desires: what he wants is *not* to want (*Ô n'y vouloir*). Because there is nothing more to drink or eat (*Ah, tout est bu, tout est mangé!*), the speaker doesn't want to live so much as he wants merely not to die. Actually, the line expresses a view of life that is even more compromised than that, since the desire not to die is qualified as a wish not to die "a little" (*un peu*), as if death were a matter of degree. Languor or weariness is taken to such absurd lengths here that we can understand why the speaker has to tell his slave Bathyllus to stop laughing (*Bathylle, as-tu fini de rire?*). Finally, even though there is nothing more to say (*Plus rien à dire!*), the speaker, who is, after all, "the Empire," manages to say three things more:

> Only, a slightly silly poem that one throws on the fire,
> Only, a somewhat dissipated slave who neglects you,
> Only, a feeling of nameless ennui that afflicts you.

1. Paul Verlaine, shown in 1891 with a glass of absinthe and an inkwell, embodies the mood evoked by "Langueur," the sonnet that helped establish decadence as a cultural movement.

Each of these lines sums up a significant aspect of decadence that we have so far identified. The first implies decadence as a form of mannered, overwrought, and therefore inferior art: the "slightly silly poem" is nothing if not excessively precious, just a collection of "indolent acrostics." The second suggests the sense of personal depravity that we associate with such emperors as Nero and Caligula, a meaning supplemented by the name Bathyllus, which by the late nineteenth century had assumed homoerotic connotations. The last line, at first, seems less specifically decadent than the other two, but the poem *is* set during the decline of the Roman Empire, which would seem to call forth a more urgent emotion than some vague "feeling of nameless ennui." These three varieties of decadence—the precious poetry, the diffident homoeroticism, and the indifference to historical decline and personal decay—were all elements of Verlaine's own brilliant but troubled career. That career took him from Paris to London and back to Paris again, where he watched the Second French Empire crumble and wrote a poem about the fall of the Roman one, where all decadence begins. So if we are to follow Verlaine's decadent itinerary, we must first go to Rome.

Chapter 1
Rome: classical decadence

"Classical decadence" is an oxymoron, or it can be: the first word suggests an ideal of balance and perfection, "a canon of acknowledged excellence" (as the *Oxford English Dictionary* [*OED*] has it), while the second word negates all that: decadence is imbalanced, imperfect, and certainly less than excellent, inferior even. As the word *canon* in the *OED* definition indicates, this opposition of perfection and inferiority is mainly literary: "*Classical* may refer specifically to the periods considered to represent the greatest flowering of both ancient Greek (Attic Greek of the 4th and 5th cent. b.c.) and Latin (1st cent. b.c. to 2nd cent. a.d.) language and civilization, but frequently refers more generally to the literature and writers of Greek and Roman antiquity as a whole." Generally speaking, the classical canon offers a model for later writers to emulate.

Literary history, and art history as well, includes a number of movements and schools that are classicistic in various senses: seventeenth-century *classicisme* in France, eighteenth-century neo-classicism in England, and the *Klassic* movement in Germany. But there is another sense of "classical decadence," one in which it is not the perfection but the decadence of antiquity that is taken as a model for later writers to emulate—and not just in their writing. When Oscar Wilde styled his hair after the fashion of the decadent emperor Nero, he was making a statement about the value that the Roman Decadence held as a model for his own appearance and behavior. That behavior included, for Wilde and others, the experience of same-sex affection that classical antiquity sanctioned, and not just in Rome. The ancient Greeks, also, accepted homosexuality as something elevated and noble, while Wilde's Victorian contemporaries regarded it as something decadent, sinful, and criminal. The love of an older man for a younger one was indeed "A Problem in Greek Ethics," as the poet and critic John Addington Symonds (1840–1893) put it in a celebrated essay. For the sympathetic Symonds, boy-love among the ancient Greeks achieved ideal, even heroic, expression principally within "the Dorian sect," which may explain Wilde's choice to name the protagonist of his only novel "Dorian." In any event, Wilde was not alone in looking to the classical period for models of decadence to emulate.

Those models were not hard to find: nineteenth-century writers could draw inspiration from both the original works of classical authors and from later commentary on those authors. The biographer Suetonius (69–122 CE) and the historian Tacitus (56–120 CE) rank high on the list of classical writers whose work inspired latter-day decadents. Both men held political positions in the Roman court and were therefore in a position to make first-hand observations and, more important, to gain access to imperial archives. Not that either writer was concerned with historical accuracy: on the contrary, they both seem to have idealized certain past leaders for their manliness and austerity—such as Augustus—and to have denigrated others—such as Nero—for their effeminacy and excess.

Several of the biographies in Suetonius's *Lives of the Caesars* bear out this pattern: the emperors Caligula, Nero, and Vitellius are all said to have had virtuous, manly ancestors but are themselves depraved, effeminate monsters (all three of these emperors either dress in women's clothing or assume the passive, "feminine" position in homosexual relations—or do both). In the case of

Caligula (r. 37–41 CE), for example, his father Germanicus is said to have been endowed with a "rich crop of virtues" that helped him behave "in the manner of our ancestors." Caligula himself, by contrast, behaves like a monster: he has incestuous relations with his sisters, feeds criminals to the arena animals because cattle are too expensive, makes parents watch the execution of their own children, and has sex with male hostages and actors, an especially shameful act because the social status of theatrical performers in ancient Rome was extremely low. So it is particularly damning for Caligula himself to have had "a stage debut" and to have danced before men "of consular rank." A comment about Caligula's dancing provides insight into Suetonius's style, which often becomes little more than a list of imperial crimes, with frequent non sequiturs: "However, despite being so multi-talented he never learned to swim."

The decadence of the dancing Caligula is easily matched by that of the singing Nero (r. 54–68 CE), another creature of the depraved stage. One of the great clichés of decadence is that "Nero fiddled while Rome burned," an expression that conveys imperial indifference to the fate of the empire and its citizens. The source of the expression is probably Suetonius, who tells us that Nero "sang of 'The Fall of Troy'" as he watched Rome burn, "dressed in his stage attire." Suetonius also tells us that Nero played the lyre (the fiddle, or violin, had not yet been invented), but it's not clear whether he accompanied himself on that instrument as he sang.

The biographer also claims that it was Nero himself who started the great fire of 64 CE, but that incendiary act seems the least of the emperor's offenses. Nero follows his adoptive father Claudius (r. 41–54 CE) not only in the imperial order of succession but also in "the murder of family members and general slaughter." He had his mother killed, and added to the crime of matricide the murder of his aunt, with any number of rivals and relatives dispatched to the underworld by means of the dagger or poison. To the emperor's crimes of cruelty Suetonius adds those of insolence, lust, luxury, and greed, but those categories seem to bleed together in the curriculum vitae of Nero's career. For example, lust and cruelty merge in the "marriage" of Nero to the boy Sporus: the emperor cuts off the young man's testicles in an attempt "to transform him into a woman, marrying him with dowry and bridal veil and all due ceremony." Nero is also credited with inventing "a kind of game, in which, disguised in the pelt of a wild animal, he would rush out of a den and attack the private parts of men and women who had been tied to stakes." Even in this bizarre sexual practice we can see what is perhaps most damning in the biography of Nero: the emperor's penchant for performance.

Strangely, Suetonius devotes as much or more attention to Nero's love of the stage, his singing, and his lyre playing as he does to his murderous cruelty and his sexual perversity. The biographer mentions that because it was forbidden for anyone to leave the theater when Nero was singing, "it is alleged that women gave birth during his shows and many who were tired of listening and applauding, when the entrance gates were all closed, either jumped furtively off the wall or pretended to be dead and were carried out for burial." A modern reader is likely to regard such remarks as funny, but Suetonius probably means to convey not humor but a sense of the emperor's absolute power over his (literally) captive audience.

The future emperor Vitellius, who ruled for less than a year during the tumultuous civil wars of 69 CE, endeared himself to Nero by presiding over one of his musical contests and claiming to represent the wishes of the crowd by calling the emperor on stage to perform. As for Vitellius's brief imperial reign, it was marked by the usual capricious cruelty—"It was his preference to impose death as a punishment on anyone and for any reason"—and by his sexual preference for actors and charioteers. But Vitellius stands out from Caligula and Nero, both of whom he admired, in his insatiable appetite. Frequent vomiting made it possible for him to enjoy at least three lavish feasts a day, sometimes four (instead of the more usual one), including such delicacies as "the livers of scar-fish, the brains of pheasants and peacocks, the tongues of flamingos, and the innards of lampreys," the latter brought by ship from Spain or Parthia (an ancient empire comprising modern Iran, Iraq, and Turkey).

Suetonius's description of Vitellius's extravagant diet is really a moral critique: the kinds of foods he eats betray a taste for foreign, specifically eastern, fare. Oriental tastes combined with "female" sexuality are used consistently throughout *The Lives of the Caesars* to describe those emperors most identified with decadence. Tacitus, also, though to a lesser degree, aligns the excesses of Vitellius with those of an "Oriental despot" in the *Histories*, the extant portion of which covers only the years 69–70 CE. This much more extensive, narrative treatment of that most gluttonous of emperors mostly confirms Suetonius's brief biographical sketch, including Vitellius's admiration for Nero. As for Nero himself, Tacitus takes up his career in the *Annals*, which covers Roman history from 14 BCE to the death of Nero in 68 CE. Writing around the same time as Suetonius, Tacitus also offers a vivid account of Nero's decadent exploits, describing, for example, his "shameful dissolution," when, dressed as a slave, the emperor wandered about Rome visiting taverns and brothels with a retinue of soldiers and gladiators to protect him.

Such exploits form a contrast with Nero's love of more refined pleasures, which Tacitus says led him to appoint a kind of consultant in matters of taste. This man's name was Petronius, whose "days were spent sleeping, his nights on the duties and delights of life." Where most men gain fame by industry, Petronius achieved celebrity because of his indolence, "and yet he was not considered a glutton and a spendthrift, like most of those who squander their fortunes, but a man of educated extravagance." We are told that this man became one of Nero's few intimate associates, so much so that the emperor "considered nothing delightful or agreeable unless it had Petronius's approval." Tacitus uses the phrase *elegantiae arbiter* (judge of elegance or taste) to describe the official duties of this Petronius, who has been identified as the author of *The Satyricon*, an important novel about first-century Rome. Scholarly opinion is divided on the question of whether Nero's *elegantiae arbiter* is, in fact, the author of *The Satyricon* known as Petronius Arbiter (the name may have been assigned to the manuscript at some later time by an anonymous copyist who had read Tacitus), but there is no doubt that the ancient novel has had an impact on modern conceptions of decadence.

The title *Satyricon* (sometimes spelled *Satyrica*) refers to satyrs, mythological creatures who were half-man, half-goat, and known especially for their lecherous behavior. So the title is a metaphor that asks the reader to imagine certain characters in the novel as lecherous or satyr-like. Some scholars also hear in the title an echo of the Latin word *satura*, "satire," a reasonable point of speculation since the novel does include both social and literary satire. The social satire is directed mostly at identifiable Roman types, such as the vulgar nouveau riche freedman Trimalchio, whose all-night banquet forms the most-often anthologized section of *The Satyricon*. The literary satire involves the parody of different types of ancient literature, including the epic. In the *Odyssey*, for example, the struggles of Homer's hero Odysseus result from the disrespect he has shown to the god Poseidon, who repeatedly frustrates him in his efforts to return from Troy to his home in Ithaca.

In *The Satyricon*, the difficulties faced by Petronius's hero Encolpius derive from some offense to the sex-god Priapus, or so it seems, given the erotic complications the hero suffers in his relationship with his beloved slave Giton and, later, with the prolonged bout of impotence he experiences with a well-to-do woman named Circe (different from the sorceress Odysseus encounters, but the name is another nod to Homer's epic). The novel may also parody ancient Greek romances, in that the eventual reunion of Petronius's homosexual heroes Encolpius and Giton seems to parallel the conventional plot of romance, whose chaste heterosexual lovers are forced by Fortune to endure trial and separation before they are finally brought together at the end. The theory of *The Satyricon* as a parody of Greek romance is disputed, but the Greek etymology of some of the names Petronius assigns to his characters might be advanced in support of the idea. The name of the hero and narrator Encolpius, for example, is Greek for "in the groin"; Encolpius's sometime rival for the affections of Giton is named Ascytlus, Greek for "unwearied" or "indefatigable" (in a sexual sense); as for Giton himself, the name means "neighbor," but with sexual connotations of availability (the boy next door); and the name Trimalchio, possibly the most decadent character in the novel, is Greek for "triply voluptuous."

Trimalchio is aptly named, since his appetite for pleasure seems easily the equal of three people. In "The Feast of Trimalchio," the lengthiest and most complete section of the fragmentary novel, Petronius paints an unforgettable picture of what the life of a decadent Roman might have been like in the age of Nero. As a prelude to the feast, Trimalchio takes exercise in the form of a ball game, urinates into a chamber pot held by a slave, and then dries his hands on the slave's hair.

The dinner itself involves multiple courses, each featuring some contrivance for the entertainment of the guests: hot sausages served on a grill over "coals" of Syrian plums and pomegranate seeds; a wooden chicken brooding over egg-shaped bread with a tiny beccafico or fig-pecker baked inside it (the little bird was a Roman delicacy); a platter featuring all the signs of the zodiac with astrologically appropriate dishes by each sign (e.g., testicles and kidneys for Gemini, the twins); a huge roast boar represented as a sow with pastry piglets suckling at its teats. When the boar is cut open, live thrushes fly out. The dessert course features a tray of cakes with a pastry Priapus as its centerpiece; when the guests bite into them, saffron juice spurts out onto their faces, a form of culinary ejaculation that the guests find richly amusing. The dinner comes to an end when the ceiling panels part and a giant hoop descends hung with golden crowns and jars of perfume, farewell gifts for the departing guests.

Suetonius mentions that the coffered ceiling of Nero's *Domus Aurea* (Golden House) included panels that would revolve to drop flowers on guests below and spray them with perfume. The imperial detail is only one of several that Trimalchio shares with this or that emperor. Suetonius also says that the emperor Claudius considered issuing an edict pardoning anyone who broke wind at table, and Trimalchio likewise forgives the flatulence of his guests. Yet it seems unlikely that Trimalchio's "imperial" qualities are meant as a satire of Nero or of any other emperor. Rather, the satire seems to be directed at the Roman type of the wealthy tradesman who adopted a lavish lifestyle and ran his household as if he *were* an emperor, however diminished or debased.

The Satyricon reminds us that the decadence of Rome has both a social and a cultural dimension. So far, we have focused on the social, on the behavior of the characters, marked mostly by excess. The fact that *The Satyricon* parodies respected literary traditions such as the epic and the romance tells us that Petronius has positioned himself outside those traditions in an effort to give cultural expression to something new and different. This combination of social decadence and artistic innovation forms a pattern that recurs in the nineteenth century: works that do not conform to established artistic traditions acquire the label "decadent" when hostile critics judge them for failing to satisfy conventional tastes. But in the Roman period this dynamic between the innovative artist or writer and the traditional critic does not really obtain: positive decadence belongs to the modern era.

When critics use the term "decadence" to describe a certain type of literature in the classical period, the meaning is almost always negative. Decadence in this negative sense usually involves the critical judgment that the writer has lavished so much attention on technique that the content has become empty. The fourth-century poet Ausonius (310–395 CE) is a good example of such a writer. He wrote a series of poems in which he set himself the purely technical task of making each line begin and end with a word of a single syllable. The trick is difficult to pull off in Latin because that language signals grammatical function by inflection, the addition of extra letters to the stem of a word depending on how it is used in the sentence (subject, object, indirect object, etc.). For example, *rex* "king" is monosyllabic as the subject of a sentence, but becomes bi-syllabic as an object: *regem*.

Ausonius compounded the difficulty by ending one line and beginning the next with the same monosyllabic word. Here is a sample, in the original Latin and an English translation, with the monosyllabic words italicized: "*Res* hominum fragiles alit et regit et perimit *fors* / *fors* dubia aeternumque labans: quam blanda fovet *spes* / *spes* nullo finita aevo: cui terminus est *mors* / *mors* avida," and so on. (*Things* that concern men are frail, prospered, guided, and destroyed by *chance*;/*chance* the unstable, ever-changing goddess, who is flattered by fond *hope*; / *hope*, who knows no bounds of time; whose only end is *death*;/*death* the insatiate ....). Even in this brief example, the excessive—and obsessive—concern with technique is obvious. Moreover, the bravura technique does nothing more that string together a collection of clichés (chance is fickle, hope is boundless, death is insatiable). Ausonius called the collection *Technopaegnion*, a Greek title that combines the words for art (*techne*) and toy (*paignion*), making the poems in it mere technical trifles, word games. Such pointless complexity deserves to be called decadent and is what Verlaine had in mind in his sonnet "Langueur" when he imagined a dissipated Roman writing "indolent acrostics" in the twilight of the empire.

The overly technical literature that Verlaine evokes and that Ausonius exemplifies, combined with the outrageous behavior that Suetonius, Tacitus, and Petronius describe, form the classical model of Roman decadence. For later commentators, the cultural and social dimensions of that model are merely symptoms—not causes—of the historical decline of the Roman Empire. The need to understand the causes of that decline became more acute in the eighteenth century, with the emergence of certain nation-states, mainly France and England, whose growth and stability depended on the successful maintenance of their colonial empires. Without question, during this period the two most influential commentators on the fall of Rome are the French moral philosopher Charles-Louis de Secondat, baron de La Brède et de Montesquieu (1689–1755), known simply as Montesquieu (the name of his estate in Bordeaux), and the British historian Edward Gibbon (1737–1794). Montesquieu's political analysis of 1734, *Considérations sur les causes de la grandeur des Romains et de leur décadence* (Considerations on the causes of the greatness of the Romans and their decline), and Gibbon's multivolume historical study of 1776–1788, *The Decline and Fall of the Roman Empire*, both include the kind of moral condemnation of imperial life that we find in Suetonius and Tacitus. In fact, what the two enlightenment authors have in common is their sense that political rule has a moral basis.

The sense of secular morality that we find in the work of Montesquieu makes him the most acute political thinker after Machiavelli. Indeed, Montesquieu is indebted to Machiavelli's analysis of the importance of raw power and ruthless opportunism in *The Prince* (1513) and other works. For that is what Montesquieu means by *grandeur* or greatness: an ability to overcome enemies through a combination of superior military power and clever calculation concerning the strategic use of that power. Montesquieu speaks of the greatness of the Romans rather than of Rome because he is a moral philosopher who understands that individuals have character and agency: the greatness of the republic or the empire is necessarily the product of the actions of soldiers and citizens, or, rather, of soldier-citizens.

The *décadence* or decline of Rome sets in when soldiers develop loyalties that are not informed by citizenship. As Montesquieu explains, the expansion of territory created the conditions for the disloyalty that led to decline: "When the domination of Rome was limited to Italy, the republic could easily maintain itself. A soldier was equally a citizen." But as the empire expanded the soldiers under the command of powerful military leaders lost their citizen spirit, "no longer the soldiers of the republic but those of Sulla, Marius, Pompey, and Caesar." The full title of Montesquieu's *Considérations* seems to imply that both the greatness and the decline of the Romans have one set of causes. Everything that contributed to the expansion of Rome also contributed to its decline. "The greatness of the empire ruined the republic," Montesquieu says, and that formulation also seems to apply to the empire itself: the grandeur that was Rome led inexorably to its decadence.

While it is usually better to translate Montesquieu's *décadence* as "decline," there are times when he uses the word to suggest personal corruption, a meaning that applies to any number of notorious emperors. Montesquieu mentions the baseness, madness, and cruelty of Caligula, Nero, Commodus, and Caracalla, for example, but the kind of corruption such emperors exemplify does not play a major role in the decline of Rome. Montesquieu does believe that the hedonistic doctrines of the Greek philosopher Epicurus (341–270 BCE), "introduced toward the end of the republic, contributed much toward tainting the heart and mind of the Romans," but he also believes that the Romans had the unique ability to compartmentalize (as we might put it today) corruption and virtue: "[W]hatever the corruption of Rome, [. . .] the strength of its institutions had been such that it preserved its heroic valor and all of its application to war in the midst of riches, indolence and sensual pleasures—which, I believe, has happened to no other nation in the world." So corruption is not one of the causes of the decline of Roman greatness, but there is another cause, in addition to the unmanageable nature of greatness itself, that led to the ruin of Rome. That cause is Christianity, an especially effective instrument of decadence in the Eastern Empire.

Although many historians would say that the Roman Empire had already fallen by the time of the Byzantine emperor Justinian (r. 527–565), Montesquieu holds that Justinian's religious zeal weakened the empire because of his attacks on those who did not conform to the faith: "He believed he had increased the number of the faithful; he had only diminished the number of men." At one point Montesquieu mentions a "celebrated author" (in fact, the Christian philosopher Pascal [1623–1662]), who avers that "he was quite content to be sick because sickness is a Christian's true condition." (This association of Christianity with decadence will be taken up again by Friedrich Nietzsche in the nineteenth century, albeit in a somewhat different context.)

The role of Christianity in the decline and fall of Rome also emerged as one of the more controversial elements of Edward Gibbon's account of the demise of the empire. In the notorious closing chapters of the first volume of his history, Gibbon offered a truly sanguine account of the rise of Christianity, noting that, whereas the theologian might "indulge the pleasing task of describing Religion as she descended from Heaven, arrayed in her native purity," the more "melancholy duty" of the historian was to "discover the inevitable mixture of error and corruption which she contracted in a long residence upon earth, among a weak and degenerate race of beings."

The association of Christianity with corruption and degeneracy, two of the bywords of decadence, prompted contemporary outrage, but Gibbon defended the assessment of the faith he had made in the first volume and went on to conclude his account of Rome's decline by doubling down on his claim that Christianity had had a corrosive effect on the empire. The core of the claim is that the Christian promise of a future life obviates the need for action in the present. Because "[t]he clergy successfully preached the doctrines of patience and pusillanimity; the active virtues of society were discouraged; and the last remains of military spirit were buried in the cloister." In arguing that Christianity contributed to imperial decline by diminishing the "military spirit" of Rome, Gibbon follows Montesquieu, who observed that "[r]eligion and empires prosper in different ways": the strength of one is bound to involve the weakening of the other. Gibbon also echoes Montesquieu when he says that "the decline of Rome was the natural and inevitable effect of immoderate greatness." But that word *immoderate* is one thing that sets Gibbon off from Montesquieu, because the English historian goes to much greater lengths than the French philosophe to explain the cruelty and excess of those emperors who did not practice moderation and so merit the epithet "decadent."

For Gibbon, the decline of Rome begins in earnest after the peaceful and prosperous reign of the two Antonine emperors, Antoninus Pius (r. 138–161 CE) and Marcus Aurelius (r. 161–180). The successor to the virtuous and stoical Aurelius was the emperor's son Commodus (r. 180–192), a monster of decadence by any measure. Gibbon observes that "[t]he monstrous vices of the son have cast a shade on the purity of the father's virtue," adding that "every sentiment of virtue and humanity was extinct in the mind of Commodus." The historian expatiates at some length on this emperor's extravagant depravity, but withholds certain details out of a sense of decency. This kind of respect for the reader is a feature of the historian's decorous and sonorous writing that is occasionally breached, but only partially, in his celebrated footnotes, where Gibbon gives the reader a taste of what lies beyond "the decency of modern language" in the classical sources.

The account of the Emperor Elagabalus (r. 218–222), who assumed power at the age of 14, is a case in point. Elagabalus (known also as Heliogabalus) is perhaps the one emperor most celebrated in nineteenth-century decadent culture, a status that derives, in part, from Gibbon's description of the young man's transvestite homosexuality: "The master of the Roman world affected to copy the dress and manners of the female sex, preferred the distaff to the scepter, and dishonoured the principal dignities of the empire by distributing them among his numerous

Gibbon's description of Emperor Commodus

[H]e valued nothing in sovereign power, except the unbounded license of indulging his sensual appetites. His hours were spent in a seraglio of three hundred beautiful women, and as many boys, of every rank, and of every province; and, wherever the arts of seduction proved ineffectual, the brutal lover had recourse to violence. The ancient historians have expatiated on these abandoned scenes of prostitution, which scorned every restraint of nature or modesty; but it would not be easy to translate their too faithful descriptions into the decency of modern language. The intervals of lust were filled up with the basest amusements. The influence of a polite age, and the labor of an attentive education, had never been able to infuse into his rude and brutish mind the least tincture of learning; and he was the first of the Roman emperors totally devoid of taste for the pleasures of the understanding.

Edward Gibbon, *The Decline and Fall of the Roman Empire* (1776)

lovers, one of whom was publicly invested with the title and authority of the emperor's, or, as he more properly styled himself, of the empress's husband." The passage is usually accompanied by a note (some editions omit it): "A dancer was made praefect of the city, a charioteer praefect of the watch, a barber praefect of the provisions. These three ministers with many inferior officers were all recommended *enormitate membrorum*," that is, on the basis of penis size. The Latin phrase masks what Gibbon's early readers might have found a breach in decency; more recently, a British wit remarked that such passages reveal that Gibbon, a life-long bachelor, "lived out most of his sex life in his footnotes."

The classical source for Gibbon's account of the strange career of Elagabalus is a collection of imperial biographies known as the *Historia Augusta* (Augustan Histories), a Latin history of the late fourth century CE. The book offers sensational but mostly spurious accounts of the emperors from Hadrian (r. 117–138 CE) to Numerian (r. 283–284 CE). The life of Elagabalus presented in the *Historia Augusta* was well known to a number of nineteenth-century decadents, including the most important decadent of them all, Joris-Karl Huysmans. In *À Rebours* (1884), Huysmans imagines Elagabalus "treading in silver dust and sand of gold, his head crowned with a tiara and his clothes studded with jewels, working at women's tasks, calling himself Empress and bedding every night with a new Emperor, picked for choice from among his barbers, scullions, and charioteers."

In Oscar Wilde's *The Picture of Dorian Gray*, the title character comes under the spell of a French novel that bears a close resemblance to that of Huysmans and is fascinated by the

Elagabalus in the *Augustan Histories*

Elagabalus frequently ate camels-heels and also cocks-combs taken from the living birds, and the tongues of peacocks and nightingales. He served to the palace-attendants huge platters heaped up with the viscera of mullets, and flamingo-brains, partridge-eggs, thrush brains, and the heads of parrots, pheasants, and peacocks. He fed his dogs on goose-livers. He sent grapes from Apamea to his stables for his horses, and he fed parrots and pheasants to his lions and other wild animals. For ten successive days he served wild sows' udders, peas with gold-pieces, lentils with onyx, beans with amber, and rice with pearls; and he also sprinkled pearls on fish and truffles in lieu of pepper. In a banqueting-room with a reversible ceiling he once overwhelmed his guests with violets and other flowers, so that some of them were actually smothered to death, being unable to crawl out to the top.

The Scriptores Historiae Augustae

unnamed hero of that novel who imitates the behavior of several emperors, including Elagabalus, who "had painted his face with colours and plied the distaff among the women." Wilde himself was drawn to a bust of Elagabalus on a visit to Naples in 1897, noting in a letter that the face possessed a "grave, somewhat severe beauty, and the most delicate refinement of type, rather like a young Oxonian of a very charming kind." Wilde's impulse to identify the boy-emperor with a student at Oxford University is of a piece with the broader tendency of the Victorians to associate elements of the Roman Empire with the British one. Usually, the Romans were held up as examples of excess to caution the British against like behavior, so Wilde departs from that pattern, finding in the face of the Roman bust "the expression of pride and *ennui*" that he has seen on the faces of his contemporaries. Wilde's contemporary Sir Lawrence Alma-Tadema also departs from the pattern in his painting of one of the more notorious episodes from the *Historia Augusta*—the moment when Elagabalus decides to smother his dinner guests with flowers.

In *The Roses of Heliogabalus*, the boy-emperor himself is recognizable as the reclining figure in a golden toga wearing a thin, golden tiara, his face lightly bearded and sporting a scant moustache, indicating adolescence. Seated next to him is his mother and, beside her, an especially dissipated member of the emperor's court, crowned with laurel and holding a wine bowl.

A group of four courtesans lounge at the far right of the painting, one of them peering around a column at a bearded young man with braided hair held in place by a jeweled hairpin. This figure, who exchanges gazes with the emperor, must be a court favorite, since he wears a massive necklace of gold chain. The homosexual nuances of the exchange of gazes are unmistakable, complemented by other same-sex dramas that appear to play out in the painting. The laurel-crowned hedonist, for example, is toasting a young man beneath him in the welter of roses, while the woman shielding herself from the cascading flowers with a large feathered fan looks

2. A detail of Sir Lawrence Alma-Tadema's *The Roses of Heliogabalus* (1888) captures a moment from the Roman decadence when the boy emperor Elagabalus smothers his guests with flowers.

intently at another woman, wearing a wreath of roses about her head, reclining on a heavily cushioned couch. The woman on the couch exchanges gazes with the viewer, thereby implicating the spectator in the florid decadence of Elagabalus. Although critics typically dismiss Alma-Tadema as a skilled technician whose paintings lack substance, *The Roses of Heliogabalus* reveals a measure of psychological complexity in the erotic regard the figures hold for one another as the extravagant scene unfolds and the less fortunate of them undergo a most luxurious death.

Another typical critique of Alma-Tadema's Rome paintings is that they are of dubious historical accuracy. What we see in his paintings are not ancient Romans, the critics say, but "Victorians in togas." While the artist went to considerable effort to incorporate details in his paintings that were consistent with the latest archaeological discoveries, much of his work does seem to transfer the life of the British leisure class onto Roman antiquity. In a strange way, then, he appears as a kind of "painter of modern life," but one rather different from the sort Baudelaire imagined.

Alma-Tadema's successful artistic career combines with the popularity of "toga plays" about ancient Rome on the British stage and with the fascination among upper-class Englishmen for the *tableau vivant*, in which they posed for the camera in Roman garb. For the most part, these types of representations suggest an identification of the British Empire with the Roman one that emphasized all the material benefits of imperial life in the late nineteenth century but none of the psychological anxieties.

An exception to this trend is *Marius the Epicurean* (1885), a novel of ancient Rome by Walter Pater. The highly aesthetic novel is set in the Rome of the Antonines, the age that Gibbon called "the period in the history of the world, during which the condition of the human race was most happy and prosperous," an assessment that contrasts with Montesquieu's criticism of the Antonines for allowing the spread of the epicurean philosophy of pleasure during their reigns. Pater's attitude toward Epicureanism is more sympathetic than Montesquieu's, but his general view of the era is a good deal more anxious and conflicted than Gibbon's. That is so because the English author treats second-century Rome as an age of social transition that reflects questions and concerns about the changing mores of his own era. At times the comparison is quite explicit: "That age and our own have much in common, many difficulties and hopes. Let the reader pardon me if here and there I seem to be passing from Marius to his modern representatives—from Rome, to Paris or London."

Pater uses Rome to explore ideas and behavior, such as the Epicurean doctrine of pleasure and male homosexuality, that would have been much more difficult—if not impossible—to address in a contemporary British setting. The aesthetic sensibility of Pater's protagonist Marius is a bridge across time, for the literature that Marius encounters in second-century Rome often finds its analogue in nineteenth-century decadent culture. *The Golden Ass*, a novel by the Latin author Apuleius, is said to possess qualities in common with "what French writers call the *macabre*—that species of almost insane preoccupation with the materialities of our mouldering flesh, that luxury of disgust in gazing on corruption." Certain scenes from Apuleius's book are deemed "worthy of Théophile Gautier," and its style seems not dissimilar to the style of decadence that Gautier himself described: "full of the archaisms and curious felicities in which that generation delighted, quaint terms and images [. . .], racy morsels of the vernacular and studied prettinesses." As for the pagan world in general, Marius is struck by "the depth of its corruption, and its perfection of form," a formula that suggests a sense of decadence that extends well beyond questions of literary style.

The most important historical novel in French with a bearing on the development of decadence has a rather oblique relationship to Rome. Gustave Flaubert's *Salammbô* (1862) is set in the ancient Phoenician city-state of Carthage in the years after 241 BCE, when the Roman Republic defeated the Carthaginians in the First Punic War and gained control of the island of Sicily. The cost of the conflict and the tribute exacted by the Romans so impoverished Carthage that it could not pay off the foreign soldiers (mainly Libyans) employed in the war, whose revolt led to a new conflict, known to history as the Mercenary War (240–238 BCE). The situation is summed up in Flaubert's novel when Hamilcar Barca, the leader of the Carthaginians, observes that "the peace with Rome [. . .] was more disastrous than a score of battles." The novel is so densely descriptive that it is hard to follow the basic narrative: Hamilcar's dogged defeat of the mercenary forces led by the Libyan Mâtho, and that same Mâtho's romantic pursuit of Hamilcar's daughter Salammbô, priestess of the moon-goddess Tanit.

As soon as it was published, the novel prompted comparisons of Flaubert to the writers of the Roman decadence, beginning with the critic Charles Augustin Sainte-Beuve (1804–1869). Sainte-Beuve complained that the subject of the novel was so remote from modern times that it could not possibly be of interest to the reader. But that, perversely, might be the point: to get the reader as far away from modernity as possible, both temporally and conceptually. Flaubert shares with his exact contemporary Baudelaire (both born 1821) a horror of progress and a hatred of modern life, with the difference that Flaubert's attitude might be the purer form of pessimism because it was not motivated by any religious animus. The anti-modern sensibility combines in *Salammbô* with an obvious relish for acts of extreme sadism, images of gruesome decay, and a style that is all but opaque to make "decadent" a meaningful description of the novel.

Flaubert's first critic Sainte-Beuve likened the style of *Salammbô* to poetry, given the author's famously obsessive attention to style. Many passages might fairly be compared to the ornate, jeweled style of fourth-century Roman poets such as Ausonius, as in, for example, this description of "precious stones contained in gold calabashes": "There were callais torn from the mountain by slingshots, carbuncles formed by lynx's urine, glossopetri fallen from the moon, tyanos, diamonds, sandastrum, beryls." The effect of exotic unfamiliarity in this example occurs many times: Hamilcar asks for "psagas"; Mâtho is appointed "schalischim"; corn is measured out in "k'hommers," millet in "hins," and dried fruit in "betzas." Flaubert was quite proud of all this arcane erudition and defended it against the attacks of professional scholars as historically accurate, an odd position in view of his refusal to ascribe any significance to history whatsoever: he judged the past, the present, and the future equally "bêtise" (stupid, one of Flaubert's favorite words).

However stupid the Carthaginians might have been, Flaubert delights in describing their extreme violence, which culminates in the death of the captive Mâtho, who runs a gauntlet of sadistic citizens who tear at his body until his appearance "is no longer human": "he was just a long shape, completely red from top to bottom." Salammbô finds the man in this mangled condition attractive, a pattern of perversity that appears in slightly different form earlier when the horribly diseased Hanno, Hamilcar's rival, gives his soldiers female captives to rape and slaughter, but reserves the most attractive women for himself, "for his appalling illness made him burn with urgent desires, which he satisfied with all the frenzy of desperation." Hanno, who suffers from leprosy, is captured and crucified by the mercenaries, a punishment that reveals "the horror of his person": "Ulcers covered his nameless bulk; the fat of his legs hid his toenails; from his fingers hung what looked like greenish strips; and the tears streaming down among the tumours on his cheeks gave his face a fearful, grievous expression, seeming to take up more room than on any other human face." Here is a real delectation of decay that perversely fetishizes the human body and asks the reader to regard the horror with a kind of cold desire.

The ornate style, the sadistic action, and the delectation of decay are all part of the disdain for modernity that makes *Salammbô* a model for the decadent sensibility. More than anything else, however, it is Flaubert's handling of history that contributes to the sense of decadence in the novel. The narrative itself embodies decadence in the way events are related: the action seems frozen in place, so much so that the static narrative can reflect only some larger disdain for progress itself. In this regard, Flaubert was typical of those of his generation whose disappointment with the failure of the 1848 revolutions led to cynicism and despair. His intense devotion to style is also typical of those writers later described as decadents. Indeed, the combination of pessimism and aestheticism makes Flaubert one of the more pertinent precursors of decadence in France. His reconstruction of the Carthaginian Empire rather than the Roman Empire as a way of expressing contemporary concerns about modernity is a bit atypical, however, since many of his countrymen saw in the decline of Rome a ready comparison to the decadence of Paris. And it is to that comparison that we now turn.

Chapter 2
Paris: cultural decadence

The decline of Rome held special relevance for the French. After all, the architects of the French Revolution, like those in America before them, took Republican Rome as their model of governance. Moreover, the French found in Napoléon a Caesar who betrayed the revolution by taking the title of emperor. In French political chronology, the First Republic (1792–1804) is followed by the Napoleonic era known as the First Empire (1804–1815), leading some historians to say that the French repeated several centuries of Roman history in just over two decades.

Even before Napoléon, the French-Roman analogy appears to have been quite insistent among the French themselves. Just as Rome experienced a Golden Age during the reign of the Emperor Augustus (r. 27 BCE–14 CE), so did France during the reign of Louis XIV (r. 1643–1715), the Sun King, with the classical poets Virgil and Horace having their latter-day French counterparts in such exponents of *classicisme* as Racine and Corneille. And if Rome had its decadence, then so did France, with the difference that the decadence of France seems to recur at regular historical intervals.

Both the rococo art and the libertine literature that marked the reign of Louis XV are decadent in comparison to the great age of neoclassical art that came before, or so goes conventional opinion. That opinion was reasserted in 1834 by the traditionalist critic

Désiré Nisard when he compared the poetry of the decadent Romans to that of his romantic contemporaries in *Études de moeurs et de critique sur les poètes latins de la décadence* (Cultural-critical studies of the Latin poets of the decadence). At the end of this book Nisard makes explicit what he had already implied throughout his study: that Victor Hugo and other romantic poets of Nisard's day had something in common with the inferior poets who wrote during the decline of Rome.

Decadence, it turns out, is a style, one that draws the reader's attention to individual words and phrases at the expense of the whole, that indulges in imaginative flourishes rather than reasoned discourse. The lack of unity and the lack of reason offer no benefit to the reader, unlike classical literature (whether Roman or French), which possesses "truths essential to the preservation of man's moral grandeur." Later, Nisard's negative criticism would be put to positive use, as attention to detail, imaginative fantasy, and the removal from morality became hallmarks of the decadent aesthetic.

After Nisard, the most important negative critique of decadence comes in visual form, in 1847, when the artist Thomas Couture captured the comparison of the Romans and the French on canvas: *The Romans of the Decadence* asks the viewer to consider anew just how completely the cultural decline of France mirrored the fall of Rome. While the artistic merits of Couture continue to be debated, his most famous painting undoubtedly illustrates some critical dimensions of decadence. From the first, the painting was regarded as both a political and a cultural allegory: Couture's contemporaries understood the scene as a representation of Roman decadence all right, with the decadent Romans standing in for the decadent French. The basic device of the painting recalls Suetonius: the statues that look down in disapproval on the florid orgy below them suggest the Roman writer's contrast of the decadent emperors' actions with those of their virtuous ancestors.

In Couture's painting, the central figure of Germanicus, the austere commander of Roman forces in the north and the father of the dissolute Caligula, makes the contrast clear. And so do the stern faces of the other statues, all completely counter to the visage of the figure identified as the Emperor Vitellius, the portly character just below the bare-breasted, gyrating dancer with her head thrown back. Possibly, the presence of Vitellius dates the orgy to 69 CE, the "year of the four emperors" when Rome was wracked by civil war. Hence, the painting becomes a prescient image of civil conflict in France, looking forward to the Revolution of 1848. That retrospective reading, however, is hard to justify given Couture's own conservative politics: his sympathies lay with the aristocracy displaced by the July Monarchy of 1830, which led him to treat the rising bourgeoisie as literally ignoble and figuratively decadent. In this regard, Couture confirms a more general tendency

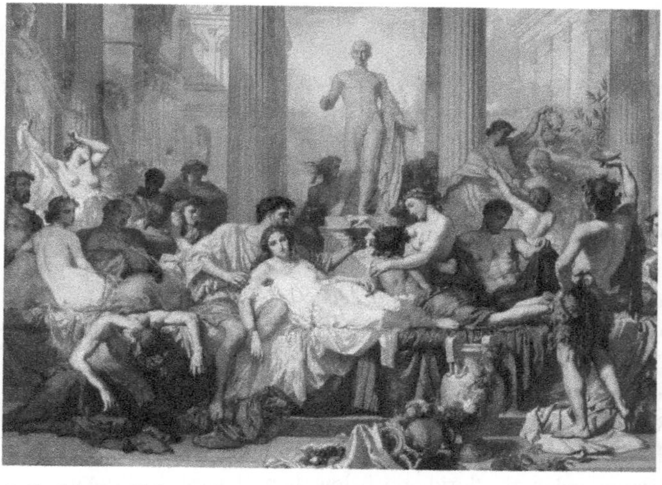

3. In this detail from Thomas Couture's *The Romans of the Decadence* (1847), the statues of the ancestors of republican Rome look down in disapproval on the decadent debauch below them.

to regard forms of social modernity as a species of decadence. But it is also true that the painting can function as an all-purpose allegory, since the dualistic contrast of noble ancestors and decadent descendants can be interpreted in a wide variety of ways.

One such interpretation is consistent with another feature of decadence that we have already identified, namely, its inherently generative dimension. In addition to making a social critique, Couture also used *The Romans of the Decadence* to make a statement about the need for a new artistic direction. In fact, the sensational canvas served as a large-scale advertisement for the new school of art that Couture himself founded the same year he exhibited it. The formal announcement for this "École de M. Couture" made the artist's eclectic aims clear: he meant "to found a school of national painting adequate to the needs of the time" that would reject both "the spurious classical school" and "that abominable school, known under the rubric of 'Romantic.'" He also rejected "petty artistic commercialism" in favor of the great art of Greek antiquity, the Italian Renaissance, and the Dutch Golden Age.

While Couture does not single out the art of ancient Rome in the prospectus for his school, *The Romans of the Decadence* obviously does, by way of the monochrome statues mostly copied from ancient marbles and bronzes. Of course, some critics would say that Couture's mannered, eclectic mixture of different artistic styles is itself an example of decadence. For this reason, Couture has not received that much credit for the revolution in nineteenth-century painting wrought by Édouard Manet, who trained in Couture's studio. Still, the Couture-Manet connection says much about the cultural dynamics of decadence. Perhaps Manet emerged as a true painter of modern life because his training put him in the position of re-thinking the worn-out conventions and traditions Couture promoted.

Why Baudelaire should have chosen the illustrator Constantine Guys as the exemplary "painter of modern life" for his 1863 essay rather than the artist Manet remains an unanswered question.

The essay was actually written around the time that Baudelaire met Manet, in 1859, the same year the artist painted *The Absinthe Drinker*, a work that breaks new artistic ground. That painting might fairly be called Baudelairean because of the paradoxical nature of the representation: the derelict man is a definite modern type, simultaneously dignified and sordid. The aesthetic kinship between the poet and the painter is undeniable, as their contemporaries recognized: one critic called Manet "the pupil of Goya and of Charles Baudelaire." What the two have in common is the sense that *all* aspects of contemporary reality, including those traditionally regarded as distasteful or forbidden, merit the same level of artistic respect. When Baudelaire writes about prostitutes, for example, or when Manet paints them, the point is not to shock but to show that such subjects are integral to the circumstances of social modernity. In his essay on Guys, Baudelaire wrote about prostitutes in the hope that some artist might one day come along who could capture their "nobility"—"even in the mire."

While we would not today describe the social issue of prostitution in such terms, in 1863 Manet seems to have been following Baudelaire's lead when he painted *Olympia*, a nude in the noble tradition of Venetian, Spanish, and French masters reclining in the "mire" of a modern brothel. One detail of the painting has been specifically identified with Baudelaire: the black cat arching its back at the far right edge of the canvas. The image might be a visual allusion to "Le Chat" (The cat), a poem in which Baudelaire describes himself stroking his cat, looking into its "agate eyes," and seeing there the same "cold, deep gaze" as the one his Creole mistress, Jeanne Duval, dark like the cat, directs at him. Although Manet is rarely considered in the context of decadence, he shares with Baudelaire a skeptical attitude toward modernity, one reflected in his paintings by the artistic choice of subjects—such as absinthe drinkers and prostitutes—that reveal the downside of progress, the negative effects of the bourgeoning, bourgeois society of both the Second Empire and the early years of the Third Republic.

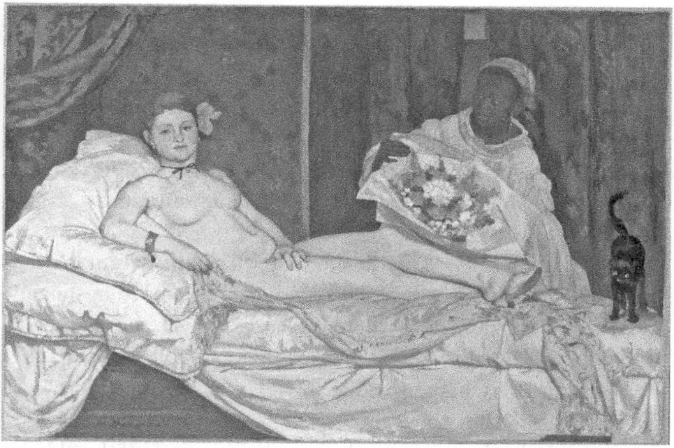

4. Manet's *Olympia* (1863) and other works by this "painter of modern life" prompted contemporary critics to call him a student of Goya and Baudelaire.

The Paris into which Baudelaire was born in 1821 still had the character of a medieval village, or collection of villages, so during his lifetime he was literally witness to the modernity that took shape all around him, when Baron Hausmann began the renovation of the city in 1853. By the time Baudelaire died in 1867, roughly 25,000 buildings had been destroyed, including the house—and the street—where the poet was born.

The vast project of urban renewal was mostly the brainchild of Charles Louis-Napoléon Bonaparte, nephew of the emperor. Elected president of the Second Republic in 1848, Louis-Napoléon engineered a coup toward the end of what was supposed to have been a single term, dissolved the Legislative Assembly, rewrote the Constitution, and established himself as Emperor Napoléon III. One of his first acts as emperor was to enlist the career bureaucrat Georges-Eugène Hausmann as Prefect of the Seine to execute the plan that would transform Paris from a medieval to a modern city.

Population growth necessitated the renovation: the industrial revolution brought thousands into the city from the countryside. From 1825 to 1850, the population of Paris grew from 855,000 to 1,314,000, making it the second-most populous city in Europe, after London. The addition of almost half a million people to Paris in a quarter century created problems that had to be addressed in the areas of public safety, transportation, and sanitation.

The renovation of Paris marks the somewhat tardy triumph of modernity over medievalism, but Baudelaire remained nostalgic for the old Paris the new one had replaced. Indeed, the characters who populate Baudelaire's poems are unimaginable as residents of Hausmann's Paris, with its wide, gas-lit boulevards and airy public parks. Rather, they seem to belong forever to the vanished warren of dark alleyways and claustrophobic spaces of the old medieval city.

Consider, for example, the poem titled "Les Sept Viellards" (The seven old men), from the *Tableaux Parisiens* (Parisian scenes) section of *Les Fleurs du mal* (The flowers of evil), the volume of poetry Baudelaire published in 1857. The poet describes a street so muddy it resembles a river, the houses that line it compared to wharves. Suddenly a bent, broken old man, dressed in rags, appears, a look of malevolence in his eye. He tramps past in the mud and slush, "as though crushing the dead beneath his clogs." Then, "from the same hell," the man's twin appears, then another, and another, until seven old men, or seven apparitions of old men, stand before the poet, who turns and staggers home, like a drunk who sees things double. Resuming the nautical metaphor that opens the poem, Baudelaire describes himself as a helmsman struggling to steer a boat without a mast in a storm, "through a monstrous, shoreless sea."

The setting of the poem is mostly hallucinatory and hardly realistic, but it is difficult to imagine the sentiments Baudelaire expresses in it being inspired by the modern Paris of Napoléon III and Baron Hausmann. Quite the contrary: the seven old men seem pretty clearly personifications of the seven deadly sins of Catholic theology, with the city itself becoming an analogue of hell. The key point here is that Baudelaire's poetic imagination involves a conflict of medievalism and modernity, a conflict that was, so to speak, manifested by the physical transformation of Paris that Baudelaire experienced first-hand. The old Paris, and its down-and-out inhabitants, were, for Baudelaire, everyday evidence for original sin, for the innate depravity of humankind.

Depravity is not necessarily decadence, but the idea of original sin that drives all of the smaller, subsidiary sins that constitute the nature of humanity as orthodox Catholic doctrine conceives it is part of the idea of decadence that begins to emerge in the nineteenth century with the growth of Baudelaire's reputation. Moreover, the conception of original sin undergirds what is perhaps the most significant element of the break with romanticism that decadence entails: the negation of the concept of nature as a positive ideal. The French romantics, following the philosophy of Jean-Jacques Rousseau, advocated a return to nature as the cure for the disease of civilization. The notion of the noble savage reflects the idea that man in a state of nature approaches perfection, not unlike Adam in Eden before the fall. Baudelaire rejected such thinking completely, insisting not only on the fact of original sin, but also on humanity's innate predisposition for self-destruction.

In "Au Lecteur" (To the reader), the poem that serves as a prologue to *Les Fleurs du mal*, Baudelaire imagines Satan as a kind of puppeteer pulling the strings that make us love the things we should find repugnant. And if we have not yet poisoned or stabbed someone, it's not because we are good, only that we are timid, afraid to act on our devious desires. As with "Les Sept Viellards," the deadly sins are again personified in "Au Lecteur," this time as animals: jackals, panthers, hounds, apes, scorpions, vultures, serpents. But among this "vile menagerie of vices" one stands out as "uglier, nastier, fouler" than the rest: "C'est l'Ennui!" Ennui or boredom is then personified as an addict of opium or hashish, "smoking his hookah" and dreaming of destruction: "He would gladly reduce the world to rubble, and swallow all creation in a yawn." Possibly, the reader knows this "fastidious monster" so well because the act of reading itself might be evidence of ennui. In any event, the reader who sits back and judges from a position of superiority the human condition Baudelaire describes will be brought up short by the poem's closing line: "— Hypocrite lecteur, — mon semblable, — mon frère!" (Hypocrite reader,— my likeness,— my brother!).

In "Au Lecteur," Baudelaire takes the anti-romantic position that human nature is fundamentally evil, not good. That reaction to Rousseau's belief in the inherent goodness of humanity is only the first part of the poet's anti-romantic agenda: the second concerns his antagonism to nature as a model for art. The romantics, of course, did not invent the idea of art as an imitation of nature, but they revived it, or, better, revitalized it as a model not only for art but also for life. To Baudelaire's mind, such thinking is not only erroneous but dangerous: the less evidence of the insidious presence of nature in both art and life, the better. In "The Painter of Modern Life," Baudelaire praises the use of cosmetics as one way to obscure or negate natural beauty; indeed, Baudelaire regards "natural beauty" as an oxymoron and says that anyone who prefers nature unadorned is degenerate.

Part of Baudelaire's thinking here is misogynistic: as the more "natural" gender, woman must do more to obscure the physical signs of innate depravity. But cosmetics is also a metaphor for art, which, in turn, assumes ethical dimensions: "Everything beautiful and noble is the result of reason and calculation. Crime, of which the human animal has learned the taste in his mother's womb, is natural by origin. Virtue, on the other hand, is artificial, supernatural [. . .] Evil happens without effort, naturally, fatally; Good is always the product of some art." Baudelaire's reversal of the romantic hierarchy of nature and art makes of nature itself something degenerative, not restorative, so there is a kind of moral imperative toward art and artifice. At the same time, the human condition is ineluctably natural: in one sense, the human animal is decadent by definition, and anyone who wishes to overcome this condition must become as artificial and refined as possible.

The book that did so much to form this idea of decadence, Baudelaire's *Les Fleurs du mal*, is dedicated to Théophile Gautier (1811–1872). The admiration Baudelaire felt for Gautier is partly due to his novel *Mademoiselle de Maupin* (1835), a work that reflects the liberated thinking of the romantic era to which it belongs. The story concerns the strange attraction that the young poet d'Albert and his mistress, Rosette, both have toward a delicate youth named Théodore de Sérannes, in reality Mademoiselle de Maupin cross-dressing as a man. The novel is not quite so scandalous as it sounds (once the gender disguise is dropped the various characters settle into their normative heterosexual roles), but it did much to ensure a place for Gautier in literary history as one of the great precursors of the decadent movement.

That status is mainly the result of its celebrated preface, a lively, irreverent attack on those critics who insisted that literature be both virtuous and utilitarian, that it should, in short, reflect the ideals of progress. Gautier points out that the proponents of progress have not really achieved as much as they claim. They have not, for example, invented a new mortal sin (there are still only seven), nor have they surpassed in cuisine the menu of Trimalchio's dinner that Petronius describes. As for literature, utilitarian progressiveness is simply beside the point, as Gautier says in what is undoubtedly the most salient paragraph of this influential preface: "Nothing is really beautiful unless it is useless; everything useful is ugly, for it expresses a need, and the needs of man are ignoble and disgusting, like his poor weak nature. The most useful place in a house is the toilet." Here is the origin of the aesthetic doctrine that came to be known as "art for art's sake," so crucial to the development of decadence in both France and England, and that Oscar Wilde was to echo more than fifty years later: "All art is quite useless."

The preface to *Mademoiselle de Maupin* combines with another of his prefaces, the "Notice" introducing the third, posthumous edition of Baudelaire's *Les Fleurs du mal* (1868), to make Gautier one of the more influential theoreticians of decadence in the nineteenth century. The importance of the essay lies in the way Gautier ameliorates the concept of decadence by drawing a distinction between a decadent poet and a poet of decadence. Like Nisard before him, Gautier describes the decadent style, which more properly should be called the style of decadence, that is, the style that is best suited to describing what life is like in a period of historical decline and social decay. Unlike Nisard, who urged a return to the clarity and reason of the classical style, Gautier stresses the need for a new style capable of expressing all the obscure, half-formed feelings that life in a decadent age entails.

Only two years after Gautier wrote his preface to Baudelaire's book, the decadence of France seemed very real indeed, with the defeat of the nation in the Franco-Prussian War of 1870. A year later, Paris descended into anarchy—and anarchism—when the Commune de Paris (municipality of Paris) seceded from the state. The fragmentation of French society in the 1870s soon led to social theories of decadence, and, once again, Baudelaire was the inspiration. In a series on "Contemporary Psychology," the critic Paul Bourget took Baudelaire as an exemplary figure of the period. Writing in 1881, he adopted the scientific language of positivism to combine Nisard's concept of the decadent style with Gautier's idea of the decadent society. Nisard had argued that a decadent style was one that emphasized smaller units of composition over the whole. Gautier had argued that the style of decadence was necessary to express what life was like in a declining empire. Bourget said that the formal markers of the decadent style were

Gautier's description of Baudelaire's style

The author of *Les Fleurs du mal* loved what is inaccurately called the decadent style, which is simply art that has reached the extreme point of maturity that marks the setting of ancient civilizations. It is an ingenious, complex, learned style, full of shades and refinements of meaning, ever extending the bounds of language, borrowing from every technical vocabulary, taking colors from every palette and notes from every keyboard; a style that endeavors to express the most inexpressible thoughts, the vaguest and most fleeting contours of form, that listens with a view to rendering them to the subtle confidences of neurosis, to the confessions of aging lust turning into depravity, and to the odd hallucinations of fixed ideas passing into mania. This decadent style is the final expression of the Word which is called upon to express everything, and which is worked for all it is worth. In connection with this style may be recalled the speech of the Lower Empire, that was already veined with the greenish streaking of decomposition, and the complex refinement of the Byzantine school, the ultimate form of decadent Greek art. Such, however, is the necessary, the inevitable speech of nations and civilizations when fictitious life has taken the place of natural life and developed in man wants till then unknown. It is no easy matter to write in this style, [. . .] for it expresses novel ideas in novel forms and uses words hitherto unheard. Contrary to the classic style, it admits of the introduction of shadows in which move confusedly the larvae of superstition, the haggard phantasms of insomnia, the terrors of night, the monstrous dreams that impotence alone stays in their realization, the gloomy fancies at which day would stand aghast, and all that the soul has of darkest, most misshapen, and indefinably horrible in the depths of its uttermost recess.

Théophile Gautier, "Charles Baudelaire" (1868)

equivalent to the political characteristics of the decadent society—in fact, one "law" governed them both. A healthy "organic" society was one in which all the individual "cells" were subordinated to the "total energy" of the whole. The "social organism" becomes decadent once individuals acquire autonomy and the unity of the organic society disintegrates. The same principle applies to language: "A decadent style is one in which the unity of the book falls apart, replaced by the independence of the page, where the page decomposes to make way for the independence of the sentence, and the sentence makes way for the word." He adds that "there are innumerable examples in current literature to corroborate this hypothesis and justify this analogy."

Bourget's theory of decadence found its greatest philosophical apologist in Friedrich Nietzsche (1844–1900), who incorporated the Frenchman's analysis of the relation of style and society into his own richly dialectical thinking on the problems of modernity. Nietzsche saw the signs of literary decadence—"The word becomes sovereign and leaps out of the sentence, the sentence reaches out and obscures the meaning of the page, the page gains life at the expense of the whole"—manifest in society as the moral basis—"freedom of the individual"—for a particular political theory: "*equal* rights for all." His point is not so much that democracy is decadent, but that systems of morality should not be used to justify political arrangements. Elsewhere, Nietzsche uses the terms *master morality* and *slave morality* to explain that the origins of morality lie in power: the masters are "good" and the slaves "evil." But Nietzsche goes further in his analysis of morality and says that those who are dominated by the strong make a virtue of their weakness through a process that he names *ressentiment* (resentment). This type of thinking results in "the morality of decadence or, more concretely, *Christian* morality."

Nietzsche ultimately defines morality quite succinctly as "the idiosyncrasy of decadents, with the ulterior motive of revenging oneself against life—successfully." Although Nietzsche began his philosophical career as an admirer of Richard Wagner, toward the end of that career he used the composer as the arch-example of both decadent morality and decadent style. The theme of redemption in Wagner's operas shows the need for the Christian "to be *rid* of himself" and so affirms the resentful sickness of slave morality. Throughout the essay on Wagner, Nietzsche uses French words and phrases—including the key term *décadence*—and compares the composer to French writers (such as the Goncourt brothers, Jules and Edmond). "*Wagner est une névrose*" (Wagner is a neurosis), he says, and links the composer quite specifically to the emerging tradition of Parisian decadence. For example, we are told that Wagner "avoided psychological motivation" by "putting idiosyncrasy in its place.—Very modern, isn't it? Very Parisian. Very *decadent.*"

Nietzsche's description of the idiosyncratic, "Parisian" nature of Wagnerian opera could almost stand as a description of that most influential example of decadence in literature, Joris-Karl Huysmans's *À Rebours*. The title has been translated both as "Against the grain," a literal translation, and "Against nature," which is more of an interpretation than a translation. True, most of the "againstness" in the novel is directed at nature, but it also adopts a contrarian attitude toward society, so much so that the novel's aristocratic hero separates himself from society altogether, choosing to live an extremely artificial life, with only his collection of rare books and fine art prints as his companions. Early in his career, Huysmans had been a disciple of Émile Zola (1840–1902), whose naturalistic school of fiction purported to use the novel to conduct social experiments. Most of these *romans expérimentals* (experimental novels) took the French working class as their social laboratory, subjecting characters to the constraints of heredity and environment that determined their lives, inevitably for the worst.

In *À Rebours*, Huysmans appears to be parodying the type of novel his former mentor Zola advocated by showing what happens when the life of an aristocratic rather than a working-class character is determined by an artificial environment instead of a naturalistic one. Huysmans's character, the Duc Des Esseintes, suffers from the requisite hereditary taint, for he is the lone remaining descendant of an ancient aristocratic family whose *décadence* has "followed a regular course" over the centuries, "with the men becoming progressively less manly." The environment he creates for himself, in a house outside of Paris in the suburb of Fontenay-aux-Roses, is artificial in the extreme, with a dining room made to look like a ship's cabin, complete with portholes, so the hero can go on imaginary voyages. Des Esseintes chooses Fontenay for its remoteness from urban life (the village is "unspoilt by rampaging Parisians"). The place would also have been remote from Baron Haussmann's urban renovations, which form the background to a comic interlude that adds evidence for the idea that Huysmans set himself to parody naturalism when he wrote the novel. Once he is settled into his new artificial environment, Des Esseintes spends much of his time daydreaming about his prior life in Paris. One such reverie concerns his amused recollection of a friend's decision to marry. While others urge the man to remain a bachelor, Des Esseintes enthusiastically counsels matrimony when he learns "that his friend's fiancée wanted to live on the corner of a newly constructed boulevard, in one of those modern flats built on a circular plan." Des Esseintes knows that the couple will need furniture specially designed to fit the circular walls of the apartment, that this expense will eventually force the couple to move to a less-costly but conventional residence, and that the custom furniture will not work in an apartment with straight walls and right-angled corners. Sure enough, the urban environment determines the marital destiny of the couple, whose life together becomes unbearable and leads to legal separation. The story is a *roman expérimental* writ small.

The most frequently cited example from *À Rebours* also lampoons the "scientific" principles of naturalism. Des Esseintes is having trouble with the decorative scheme of his dining room: the iridescent Oriental carpet on the floor requires some kind of contrast to heighten its "gleaming tints." On a shopping expedition to Paris he happens upon a huge tortoise displayed in the window of an up-market food shop. He buys the creature and has it delivered, but when the natural colors of the tortoise's shell fail to achieve the right aesthetic effect, Des Esseintes has the shell glazed with gold, then encrusted with precious jewels in a floral pattern derived from a Japanese print. He is quite pleased with the effect, but it is not long until the hapless reptile dies, unable "to bear the dazzling luxury imposed on it." The episode is easy to read as a naturalistic allegory of what lies in store for Des Esseintes himself, whose fantastically artificial environment and life of dazzling luxury eventually sicken him and force an ironic return to Paris for the sake of his health. That interpretation, however, seems far less interesting than the display of extreme aesthetic eccentricity the episode captures.

The same chapter contains another such display featuring Des Esseintes's "mouth organ," a collection of liqueurs to which the character has assigned various musical attributes, so that, for example, he can "taste" the sound of the flute by drinking crème de menthe and anisette, "at once sweet and tart, soft and shrill." Here, Huysmans parodies *symbolisme* (symbolism), another literary school contemporary with naturalism. The symbolist poets, following the example of Baudelaire's sonnet "Correspondances," explored the concept of synaesthesia, the idea that sensuous experiences are interchangeable to the point that one sense, such as smell, can be triggered by another sense, such as sight. In his famous sonnet, Baudelaire says that "sounds, smells, and colors correspond": some perfumes smell as fresh as a baby's skin feels or as sweet as an oboe sounds. Des Esseintes's mouth organ takes the Baudelairean doctrine of correspondences to an absurd extreme when the character contemplates playing a string quartet in his mouth, "with the violin represented by an old brandy," for example, and "the viola simulated by rum." The absurdity is elevated when Des Esseintes decides not to "listen to the taste of music" and settles on a glass of Irish whiskey, the taste and odor of which lead somehow to a daydream about the sordid experience of having a rotten tooth pulled by a lower-class dentist. In other words, a synaesthetic, symbolist stream of associations leads to the kind of squalid, slice-of-life episode typical of a naturalistic novel.

But Huysmans does more in *À Rebours* than simply parody the literary trends of his age: he also offers some genuine critical insights. The critical commentary comes by way of the character, as Des Esseintes reflects on the different writers who appeal to him, Baudelaire most of all. He admires the poet for the "morbid psychology" that makes exhaustive examination of human depravity possible and allows exploration of "those districts of the soul where the monstrous vegetations of the sick mind flourish." *Les Fleurs du mal* is usually translated "the flowers of evil," but Huysmans reminds us of the ambiguity that attaches to the word *mal*: it also means "sickness" (as in *mal*ady). Hence Des Esseintes also admires Baudelaire for expressing "the unhealthy conditions of weary spirits and melancholy souls" in paradoxically healthy terms (that is, in clear, precise diction).

It goes almost without saying that the authors Des Esseintes admires for their morbid interests write in the decadent style Gautier identified in Baudelaire. When Huysmans describes the decadence of his own times, he makes the same comparison with ancient Rome that Gautier did, the only difference being "that the decomposition of the French language had occurred suddenly and speedily." For Des Esseintes, the poets Paul Verlaine and Stéphane Mallarmé and the novelists Jules and Edmond de Goncourt best exemplify the French decadence because they all write in what Huysmans calls "the gamey style." In French, "the gamey style" is "le style faisandé," the adjective *faisandé* derived from *faisan*, "pheasant." The phrase is really a metaphor that conveys a type of taste that is simultaneously elegant and depraved, refined and corrupt: pheasant and venison are the kind of food found on aristocratic tables, but when such food is gamey, or *faisandé*, it is starting to turn, on the point of going rotten. Earlier in the novel, Huysmans uses the word *faisandage* (gaminess) to describe the literary language of fourth-century Rome, "as it decomposed like venison, dropping to pieces at the same time as the civilization of the Ancient World, falling apart while the Empires succumbed to the barbarian onslaught and the accumulated pus of ages." Here again we see the correspondence of literary and social decay that formed the basis of Nisard's negative polemic and Bourget's more neutral analysis, only now it is presented as an object of positive appreciation. Decay, in short, has become desirable.

Like Baudelaire, Huysmans was also a perceptive critic of contemporary art and was one of the first to appreciate the hard-to-classify paintings of Gustave Moreau. The difficulty of classification is part of the painter's appeal: he is simply unlike anyone else, a "unique figure in contemporary art," with no antecedents and no successors. The other part of Moreau's appeal, for Des Esseintes, is his removal from modernity. The paintings Des Esseintes most admires are *Salome Dancing before Herod* and *The Apparition*, both first exhibited in 1876. The biblical story of King Herod's daughter-in-law dancing before the king at her mother Herodias's insistence is extremely sparse in its details (not even the name Salome appears, supplied later by the first-century Jewish historian Josephus): the girl's dancing so pleases the king that he says he will give her whatever she wants, and her mother tells her to ask for the head of John the Baptist.

This spare narrative becomes, for the decadents, a misogynistic allegory of female temptation and cunning. In Huysmans's telling, Moreau's static painting is animated with erotic energy: as Salome begins the "lascivious dance" meant to arouse the "dormant senses" of the old king, "her breasts rise and fall, the nipples hardening at the touch of her whirling necklaces." Clearly, the dance is mainly in the mind of the beholder, the "potent depravity" of the dancer "accessible only to brains shaken and sharpened and

5. Gustave Moreau's numerous representations of Salome, as in this drawing of the biblical heroine performing a rather static dance, helped establish the figure as paragon of female depravity.

rendered almost clairvoyant by neurosis." Gautier also used the word *névrose* to signal the decadent sensibility in his essay on Baudelaire, and it is clear that in his description of Moreau's painting Huysmans means to do for the artist what Gautier did for the poet. Gautier said that Baudelaire revolutionized the language of poetry by "borrowing from every technical vocabulary, taking colors from every palette and notes from every keyboard." Huysmans says that Moreau extended the frontiers of painting by borrowing "from the writer's art its most subtly evocative suggestions, from the enameller's art its most wonderfully brilliant effects, from the lapidary's and etcher's art its most exquisitely delicate touches." The analysis can serve as a broader description of the hybrid, eclectic aesthetic that informs the art of decadence.

The "plot" of *À Rebours* is mostly memory: the action is almost wholly recollected, including Des Esseintes's sexual exploits. Mainly because of the sensational accounts of the sex lives of the emperors by unreliable Roman historians, decadence is often imagined in sexual terms that are perverse, excessive, or both—as in Suetonius's story of Nero covered in the pelts of wild beasts ravenously attacking the genitals of both men and women. Nothing so sensational makes its way into Huysmans's novel, but it does include a few accounts of Des Esseintes's sex life that are decadent for different reasons: impotence and exhaustion. In his youth the hero experienced traditional affairs, keeping mistresses "famed for their depravity," but he soon wearies of normative depravity and begins to indulge in "unnatural love affairs and perverse pleasures." So we are told in the prologue to the novel, and it is not until chapter 9 that we get a sampling of these affairs. There are three of them. The first involves a muscular female American acrobat called Miss Urania, whom Des Esseintes pursues because, he thinks, his feebleness will perfectly complement the hefty young woman's strength: "he got to the point of imagining that he for his part was turning female." But he is disappointed: Miss Urania is, after all, an American, and proves to be "positively puritanical in bed." The next recollected affair concerns a female ventriloquist who can throw her voice when Des Esseintes is in bed with her to create the illusion that the woman's outraged husband is at the door of the bedroom, threatening to catch his wife in flagrante delicto. Des Esseintes derives "extraordinary pleasure from this panic-stricken hurry of a man running a risk, interrupted and hustled in his fornication."

The third affair begins when he runs into a young man on the street who asks Des Esseintes for directions to the Rue de Babylone. Now, that street actually existed in the Paris of Huysmans's day, and does so still, but the way the encounter plays out suggests that Babylon, the name of the ancient city with biblical associations of luxury and corruption, is some kind of homosexual code. The chance meeting leads to a "mistrustful friendship" lasting for several months that Des Esseintes recalls with a mixture of horror and delight: "never had he run such risks, yet never had he known such satisfaction mingled with distress." Although homosexuality was not against the law in France as it was in England at the time, social stigma still attached to same-sex relations, especially among men of different social classes, as would have been the case with the aristocratic Des Esseintes and the "poorly clad" young man who accosts him, obviously lower down on the social scale. While the last affair that Des Esseintes recollects is overtly homosexual, details of the other two also suggest same-sex attraction: the ventriloquist parts her hair "like a boy's," and the physical description of Miss Urania is such that she appears to be "an integral, unmistakable man." Besides, the term *uranian* was used in the nineteenth century to describe same-sex affection as a higher, more heavenly form of love (from Latin *ūrania* "heavenly") than heterosexual attraction. Also relevant to all three relationships is a sense of inversion, another term used in the nineteenth century to describe homosexuality (as an "inversion" of "normal" sex), because in all three Des Esseintes assumes a sexual role traditionally assigned to women. Given the broader logic of the novel, this would be sex *à rebours*.

The gender reversals and inversions that form only a small part of *À Rebours* are treated much more fully in another novel first published in 1884: *Monsieur Vénus* (Mister Venus), by Marguerite

Eymery Vallette (1860–1953), who wrote under the pen name Rachilde. *Monsieur Vénus* is the story of Raoule de Vénérande, an aristocratic woman who develops a complicated attraction for one Jacques Silvert, a commoner who makes dresses and artificial flowers—occupations traditionally associated with the *grisette*, a working-class woman who supplemented her meager income with prostitution. Raoule often dresses as a man and calls Jacques her mistress, treating him as a kept woman by setting him up in an artist's studio with all the requisite bohemian trappings. Jacques's body is frequently feminized: "the curve of his back" is compared to that of the Venus Callipyge; his round thighs "make his sex uncertain"; and his high calves somehow give "prominence to his bust." But these gender reversals are often unexpectedly reversed, as when Raoule, "her brain reeling before a young man as weak as a girl," insists, "Jacques, you are master here."

Traditional male-female power relations are undermined, to say the least, when a woman masquerading as a man tells a feminized boy that she wishes to be mastered by his weakness. Later, conventional gender roles become even more unstable when the Baron de Raittolbe, a former military officer and a paragon of masculinity, confronts Jacques, his rival for Raoule's love. Struck by Jacques's white skin and full buttocks, the Baron experiences an hallucinatory wave of attraction accompanied by a violent physical reaction: "his mustache stood on end, his teeth clenched, a shudder convulsed his body, and he broke out with cold perspiration." He is almost frightened as he mutters, "I'll be damned if it isn't Eros himself." The Baron's moment of homosexual panic has all the earmarks of an hysterical attack, itself a gender reversal, which ultimately leads the Baron to challenge the boy to a duel. When Jacques is killed, Raoule is distraught, but she consoles herself by having a German craftsman fabricate "a wax figure covered in transparent rubber" that incorporates her lover's hair and eyelashes, as well as his teeth and fingernails. The artificial body is really an automaton geared to perform specific erotic functions. When Raoule embraces it and kisses it on the mouth, "[a] hidden spring, installed at the inside of the hips, connects with the mouth and brings it to life." Although necrophilia is not really new, the addition of the artifice wrought by Rachilde makes it seem so, as if to counter Gautier's comment that no one had invented a new sin since the Romans.

Verlaine praised Rachilde for her innovative efforts and said that anyone credited with the creation of a new vice should be regarded as a benefactor to society. But such "progressiveness" was belied by Rachilde's social conservatism, quite paradoxical in view of the wildly liberated behavior of her heroines. She may have dressed in men's clothes and presented herself with a calling card reading "Rachilde: homme de lettres" (Rachilde: man of letters), but she also wrote a pamphlet titled "Why I Am Not a Feminist" (1928), explaining that she had "never had any confidence in women." Her own cross-dressing she excused by saying that "my tendency to adopt a masculine style has never tempted me to claim rights which do not belong to me." "Mademoiselle Baudelaire," as some contemporaries called her, proved an apt epithet: Rachilde was like Baudelaire in both her pursuit of literary controversy and her resistance to social progress. She was also like the career bureaucrat Huysmans and the schoolteacher Mallarmé in that her decadence was mostly confined to the literature she wrote. Such cultural decadence is typical of the Parisian variant during the 1880s, with the obvious exception of Verlaine, whose decadence was both social and cultural. The decadents of London in the 1890s may not have taken their inspiration exclusively from Verlaine, but decadence in that city took a definite social turn that made it more than just a style of writing: it was also a way of life.

Chapter 3
London: social decadence

British decadence takes form in the late nineteenth century as both a reflection of and reaction to the urban plan of its capital city. London decadence has this in common with Parisian decadence, but with several significant differences. For one, London had a population double that of Paris; in fact, with a population of almost six and a half million people by the end of the 1890s, it was the largest city in the world. Another difference lies in the way the two cities allocated urban space to variations in social class. Baron Hausmann's plan pushed the poor to the perimeters of the city, creating a mostly bourgeois center. In London, the absence of any plan on the scale of Hausmann's left in place a patchwork city of neighborhoods, with the aristocracy primarily residing in West End enclaves such as Mayfair and the poor confined to East End areas such as Whitechapel (haunt of Jack the Ripper).

This urban geography is mapped fairly precisely over the best-known narrative of London decadence, Oscar Wilde's *The Picture of Dorian Gray*. The title character resides on Grosvenor Square, one of the more fashionable addresses in Mayfair, but he also consorts with criminals and opium addicts in the East End area known as Blue Gate Fields. Dorian's face remains unmarked by the crimes he commits, while his painted portrait, locked away in an attic room, ages and decays. The secret presence of the portrait in a Mayfair mansion perhaps conveys in metaphorical form all the Whitechapel problems, including murderous crime and opium addiction, that most of West End London sought to avoid.

Beginning with the Housing Act of 1885, city planners embarked on a series of ad hoc rebuilding efforts to rid the city of its numerous slums, but they contemplated nothing on the scale of the urban renovation that Hausmann oversaw. That massive undertaking points to another difference between the two cities with implications for the meaning of decadence in London. In Paris, medievalism and modernity were in conflict: the old city was forced to give way to the new, and the strongest voices of the emerging decadent sensibility—such as those of Baudelaire and Huysmans—expressed no small measure of discontent with the progressive era unfolding around them.

This conflict is less evident in responses to the built environment of London, partly because the changes were less sweeping than in Paris, and partly because the architects of the greatest building project of nineteenth-century London took medievalism itself as their inspiration. Charles Barry and A. W. N. Pugin based their neo-Gothic design for the Houses of Parliament (1836–1868) on the Collegiate Church of St. Peter at Westminster, better known as Westminster Abbey. For centuries, Westminster Abbey had served as the coronation church for British monarchs as well as the venue for royal weddings and funerals, so it made good nationalistic sense to adopt a neo-Gothic design for the Houses of Parliament to signal continuity between Great Britain's monarchal past and its parliamentary future. That future was largely imperial, another signal difference between Great Britain and France with implications for the culture of decadence in each nation.

While France had seen a succession of republics and empires come and go over the course of the nineteenth century, and had experienced the double debacle of the Franco-Prussian War and comparative method as both patriotic and cosmopolitan; nationalism is sanctified as Europeanism.

Whatever the prejudices inherent in the term, Goethe's coinage of *Weltliteratur* marks a watershed in the history of comparative literature. It matters little that he was not, in fact, the first to use the word; that honour goes to his friend Christoph Martin Wieland (1733–1813), and for all we know to others before him. What matters is rather that Goethe was *perceived* as having coined the term, thereby conferring his Olympian prestige on it. With the publication of Eckermann's conversations with Goethe in 1836, 'World literature' as a concept was launched.

The extreme capaciousness of the term—its great strength but arguably also its greatest weakness—rapidly came to apply to 'literature' as well as to the 'world'. Just twenty years later, in 1848, it turned up in the most unlikely of places: *The Communist Manifesto*. With the colonization of trade and industry by the cosmopolitan middle-classes, claim Marx and Engels, 'national one-sidedness and narrow-mindedness become more and more impossible, and from the numerous national and local literatures there arises a world literature'. The authors suggest an implicit parallel between commodities and texts, both of which now circulate, in the mid-19th century, with complete disregard for national boundaries. This may seem a radical redeployment of the aesthetic idea of *Weltliteratur*, but in fact already in 1827 Goethe repeatedly reaches for the language of 'value' (both in his conversations with Eckermann and elsewhere), speculating on rising markets in China and Serbia before returning to the gold standard of Ancient Greece.

Understood in its historical context, this conflation of commercial and cultural modes of circulation is hardly surprising. Economic metaphors of value and circulation define the mid-19th century imagination: the great Realist novels of the 1850s and 1860s by Dickens, Flaubert, or Tolstoy import capitalist models of accumulation into the sphere of culture, with the hero of the *Bildungsroman* acquiring his stock of cultural capital in order to move up in society. Yet we need not necessarily interpret models of commerce in the pejorative sense that we might now attribute to the 'commercial' exploitation of culture. In the case of Goethe, for instance, one can understand the metaphor of the 'marketplace' positively, in the Enlightenment sense of a forum for international exchange, the currency of which is as much cultural as commercial. Here as elsewhere, then, the models of comparison must themselves be approached comparatively.

What metaphors of value also convey, however, is the sheer multiplicity of Modernity, the proliferation of meaning brought about by the industrial and technological revolution. 'There was never such a miscellany of facts', writes Emerson in an essay of 1850 on Goethe as a 'representative man'.

> The world extends itself like American trade. We conceive Greek or Roman life, life in the Middle Ages, to be a simple and comprehensible affair; but modern life to respect a multitude of things.

If comparison imposed itself as an inevitable consequence of this proliferation of perspectives, so, interestingly, did a conservative recursion to the canon. In a period threatened by such uncontrollable forces, the literary mind retreated to tried and tested values: at the precise mid-point of the 19th century, Emerson's list of 'representative men'—Plato, Swedenborg, Montaigne, Shakespeare, Napoleon, Goethe—carefully circumscribes the limits of the Western world. In place of the Pillars of Hercules (see Figure 7), Emerson erects the pillars of hermeneutics, as markers of the known, decidedly European world.

This is not to say that comparative literature was exclusively the province of White Anglo-Saxon Protestants. By the 1870s,

7. The Pillars of Hercules as depicted on the frontispiece to Francis Bacon's *Novum Organum* (1620).

comparative literary studies were beginning to emerge on the far eastern edge of Europe. In 1872—the same year in which George Smith published his version of *Gilgamesh*—the University of Moscow opened a Department of World Literature; in 1875, St Petersburg followed suit with a Neo-Philological Society. The presiding spirit behind this latter initiative was a literary historian by the name of Aleksandr Veselovsky (1838–1906), who would go on to become arguably the single most important figure in the development of comparative literature in Russia. Veselovsky pioneered the study of international patterns of influence as a way of understanding national modes of development. Interested in particular in folklore and fairytales, Veselovsky used comparative methods to explore the relationship between East (Russia) and West (Europe). His study of *The Western Influence in New Russian Literature* first appeared in 1881; by 1916 it had gone through an impressive five editions, indicating its wide reception.

Veselovsky's view of comparative literature as the study of sources and influences derives its importance from the historical context of late 19th-century Russia. For Veselovsky, as for many of his contemporaries and compatriots—the generation of the so-called Silver Age—Russia was a culturally backward continent that could only develop by looking to the West. The progress of Russian culture could be charted, he believed, by comparing it to that of Western Europe. Ultimately, this would be to Russia's advantage, since the very receptivity of Russian culture would ensure that it became ever richer and stronger. Through incorporating international influences, the national culture would emerge as a fuller version of itself. Here as elsewhere—the argument re-emerges in Oswald de Andrade's 'Manifesto Antropófago' (1928), for instance, which proposes that Brazil should 'cannibalize' Europe in order to absorb its cultural nutrients—comparative literature functions as an exercise in nation building.

It is worth pausing for a moment to reflect on what this implies. If comparative literature as it was practised in 19th-century Europe emerged as the continuation of international relations by other means, this took two principal forms: empire building and nation building. The former model applied to the nations that were politically and militarily dominant, above all England and France; the latter, to those that were struggling to articulate their own identity on the international stage—here one might think of Russia or Denmark. (Germany, the country from which so much of the impetus for comparative literature emerged, occupies a pivotal position between the two models, since although it only emerged as a nation in 1871, it had long occupied a leading position culturally.) In literature as in politics, the dominant nations were aggressively expanding their sphere of influence—often in the form of large, multilingual empires—while the emerging nations were engaged in more defensive attempts to establish the importance of their own cultures through comparing them to others. Literature, to return to the economic metaphors of currency and value that define *Weltliteratur*, was a version of cultural capital, to be acquired and invested through international exchange.

One of the more interesting consequences of this is that it is often cultures perceived as 'marginal' that are more genuinely comparative, for the simple reason that they have more to gain from international cooperation. Russian Symbolism at the end of the 19th century is a case in point, drawing as it does on Schopenhauer and Nietzsche in Germany, Mallarmé and Verlaine in France, Pater and Wilde in England, and Ibsen and Strindberg in Scandinavia. Writing in the preface to the 1896 edition of *The Western Influence in New Russian Literature*, Veselovsky notes that 'respect [...] for European culture has gradually arisen', and that the field of comparative literary studies has developed commensurately from 'isolated workers' to 'friendly collective labour'. By the early 20th century, then, it is no surprise that the poet Osip Mandelstam can diagnose a 'yearning for world culture' as a constituent element of his generation's poetry. For comparative virtue emerges from cultural necessity: the great advantage of coming from the perceived margins of international culture—an advantage that obtains to this day—is that it makes possible the synthesis of existing trends. Looked at from this perspective, comparison is the privilege of posterity.

Discipline and publish

The years 1870–80 saw the emergence of comparative literature as a discipline not only in Russia, but also elsewhere in Europe. In Denmark, the literary critic Georg Brandes sought to overcome the Scandinavian cultural cringe towards continental Europe by developing a comparative method that both appropriated and alienated foreign literature. Brandes' image of the telescope—'one end magnifies, the other reduces'—neatly captures the ambivalence of his relationship to the dominant European traditions: on the one hand, he admired major writers of the continent such as Anatole France or Friedrich Nietzsche, publishing prolifically on them; on the other hand, he dreamed of establishing Danish literary figures as their equal. His celebration of the 'Men of the Modern Breakthrough'—the phrase that has come to define the Danish modernists of the late 19th century—can be understood in this light, as an attempt to harness comparative literature to the defence of minority languages. For a critic as ambitious as Brandes, to bring together the Nordic and continental traditions was a natural aspiration; like so many of the leading theories of comparison, however, it was not without national self-interest.

The tendency for comparative literature to develop at the margins of dominant cultures—but also to be recuperated by them—is nowhere more vividly apparent than in the work of Hugó Meltzl (1846–1908). Meltzl's very name—he is variously given as Hugó Lomnitzi or Hugó Meltzl de Lomnitz—suggests the 'principle of polyglottism' with which he has become associated. Born in a part of Hungary that is now Romania, Meltzl grew up speaking German under the Austro-Hungarian empire—in an area, more specifically, that ever since Bram Stoker's *Dracula* indelibly evokes what one might term 'the internal Orient' of Europe: Transylvania. Having trained in Heidelberg, in 1872 Meltzl returned to Transylvania to a professorship in German, at the age of just 26. Five years later, in 1877, he would found the first journal of comparative literature anywhere in the world.

The story of this journal tells us much about the status of comparative literature in these seminal years of the discipline. Working with an older colleague, the professor of comparative philology Samuel Brassai, Meltzl conceived the idea of a truly cosmopolitan publication. The title itself—*Acta Comparationis Litterarum Universarum*—was originally given in three languages (Hungarian, German, and French) before settling into the transnational solution of Latin; contributions, the editors declared, could be submitted in no fewer than ten official languages. Perhaps inevitably, the practice did not quite live up to the theory, with over two-thirds of the essays being published in either Hungarian or German. Equally inevitable, no doubt, was the very limited success to which such an ambitious enterprise was fated, with no more than a hundred copies ever being circulated. Indeed it is in many ways amazing that the journal lasted as long as it did, running for eleven years before shutting down, under pressure from rival publications, in 1888.

From the disciplinary perspective, however, the founding and the closing of *Acta Comparationis* tell an eloquent story. Meltzl's manifesto for the journal, published in the first issues of 1877, calls for comparative literature—understood, in the manner of the 19th century, as touching upon 'philosophy, aesthetics, even ethnology and anthropology'—to become a fully established academic discipline. Meltzl defines this discipline in contrast to literary history, which has become little more, he argues, than a tool for cultural nationalism. His 'comparative principle', on the other hand, was to have two main poles of interest, namely translation and *Weltliteratur*—the latter understood not in the jingoistic sense of German literary historians, but in the true Goethean sense as 'nothing less than the emerging discipline of the future: Comparative Literature'.

This new discipline should be driven, Meltzl declares, by the 'principle of polyglottism' (see Box 5). Abjuring 'foggy, cosmopolitanizing theories' of comparative literature, the principle of polyglottism represents the direct commerce of texts between themselves, the hope that nations as disparate as Hungary, Portugal, Germany, and Iceland might talk to each other in their own languages. If this ambition seems hopelessly impractical, a Borgesian dream of universal communication, it was designed to protect the lesser languages and to ensure that more marginal literary traditions might also maintain a voice. The journal's aim,

Box 5 'Principle of Polyglottism'

In his manifesto of 1877, Meltzl defines the principle of polyglottism in contrast to the principle of translation: where the latter is confined to the *indirect* commerce of literature, the former insists on *direct* commerce between literatures. Meltzl thereby sketches out two basic modes of comparison, modes that would be foundational for the development of comparative literature over the subsequent century. If translation involves intermediaries, polyglottism seeks unmediated access to foreign cultures, bringing them together in a Babel of competing tongues. The utopian impracticality of such an ambition—how many comparatists can read more than even a handful of languages?—is only partially mitigated by Meltzl's concession that, in practice, his journal should limit itself to ten languages, namely those that have achieved 'classicism'. That all of these languages were European is typical of the late 19th-century view of comparison: when Asian literature finally accepts 'our' alphabet, declared Meltzl, it will be worthy of inclusion.

in short, was to form 'a small polyglot parliament on various problems of Comparative Literature'.

The reality of the discipline, however, soon punctured Meltzl's pathos. In 1887, the German scholar Max Koch announced a new journal in Berlin, with the suspiciously familiar title *Zeitschrift für vergleichende Literaturgeschichte*. That the German version of *Acta Comparationis* was *Zeitschrift für vergleichende Literatur* was no coincidence; Koch was muscling in on Meltzl's territory. Beyond the usual petty academic rivalries, the struggle between the two journals matters because it illustrates the power structures underlying the development of comparative literature: from the margins of the German-speaking world, Meltzl attempts to focus attention on more international, polyglot modes of comparison; but the empire soon strikes back, declaring, from the privileged vantage point of the world city Berlin, that 'German literature and the advancement of its historical self-understanding' will henceforth form the centre of comparative interests. From minor rebellion to major repression, comparative literature advances in zigzags between the peripheries and the centres.

After the first dedicated journal, the first full-length book on comparative literature did not take long to arrive. Once again the biographical details reinforce the sense of a discipline at the margins: the Dublin-based lawyer Hutcheson Macaulay Posnett (1855–1927) published his study in 1886, just as he was emigrating to New Zealand. The author's call, in his preface, for the establishment of Chairs in comparative literature 'at the leading universities of Great Britain, America, and the Australian Colonies' suggests both the pedagogical and political context within the English-speaking world; if the subject was as yet unestablished, its potential reach was vast, indeed imperial. The harvest, in Posnett's words, was 'plenteous'.

The history of this harvest goes back, Posnett holds, as far as Dante's *De Vulgari Eloquentia* (*c.*1302), a treatise on the importance of the vernacular ironically written in Latin. Dante's subsequent decision to write the *Divine Comedy* in contemporary Italian marks, for Posnett, the beginning of the 'modern comparative science'; the subsequent rise of the continental nation-states encouraged cultural competition within Europe, while the discovery of the New World sharpened the sense of contrasts lurking outside of it. All these developments, argues Posnett in the teleological manner of the day, culminated in the Victorian era; modern scholarship was crucially now *aware* of the need for comparison, rather than pursuing it unthinkingly. 'We may call *consciously* comparative thinking the great glory of our nineteenth century.'

Posnett's historicization of comparison aside, perhaps the most interesting aspect of his study from a disciplinary perspective is its attempt to establish comparative literature as a science. We are so used to thinking of it as part of the Humanities that this conception of the discipline comes as a surprise to the modern reader. Yet *Comparative Literature* was published as part of an 'International Science' series, and indeed Posnett's whole method constitutes an attempt to establish what amounts to a sociological approach to comparative literature. Tracing the development of literary culture from clan to city, from nation to 'cosmopolitan humanity', Posnett emphasizes what he terms 'the relativity of literature', the ways in which its inflections change as society changes. Out of this evolution emerges world literature, understood as a product of ever more universal social forces.

As the discipline started gathering pace in the 1890s, Posnett's historical, evolutionary model of comparative literature quickly found supporters. Ferdinand Brunetière (1849–1906), one of the most influential figures in the French school, took the idea of evolution literally, developing, in a study of lyric poetry, an explicitly Darwinian model of the growth and decay of literary genres. In a lecture of 1900, he applied this model to national literatures more broadly, claiming that comparison is as much successive as simultaneous, since nations take turns to dominate European culture: Italy from 1450 to 1600; Spain from 1600 to 1670; France from 1660 to 1750; England from 1720 to 1820; Germany from 1820 to 1870. Yet by the end of the 19th century, argues Brunetière in a manner that anticipates the debates of some hundred years later, the hegemony of Europe had to be put in a broader perspective: 'European literature is only a branch, or better yet a province, and maybe even a narrow province, in the almost infinite field of comparative literature.' The global ambition of the discipline was becoming increasingly apparent.

This ambition was also starting to manifest itself on the other side of the Atlantic. Over the course of the 1890s, the first Chairs of comparative literature were founded at the Ivy League universities; in a sign of the increasing self-confidence of the discipline, pioneers such as Charles Mills Gayley (1858–1932) started agitating for the creation of an American 'Society of Comparative Literature'. In an essay of 1903, Gayley argues for a largely historical, sequential understanding of comparison: 'first the history of each literature; then the historic relations between literatures. That in turn is followed by the synthesis in literature as a unit.' If the model is still recognizably that of the 19th century—emphasizing the importance of anthropology and concluding that comparative literature amounts to 'literary philology'—it is also recognizably European in the way it builds a process of development into literary history. At the dawn of the new century, that is to say, for better or for worse Europe was still the cultural centre of comparison.

The crisis of the 'European mind'

As the 'long nineteenth century' drew to a close in the years leading up to World War One, the colonial model of comparison—with intellectual fashions radiating out from Europe like spokes from a wheel—came to a head. The rise of modernism in the early decades of the 20th century heralded a renewed focus on internationalism in literature and literary criticism. Despite the vital impulses it received from American expatriates such as Ezra Pound and T.S. Eliot, modernism was in many ways the last great European movement, a swansong to the high culture of the continent. From Russian formalists to Italian futurists, from French surrealists to German expressionists, the avant-garde circulated—and collaborated—across Europe. Inevitably, comparative literature came to reflect this.

For all the internationalism of the modernist era, however, it is striking just how little the term 'comparative' is actually used at this time. Anthologies of the discipline struggle to find explicit statements of comparison from this period, for the simple reason that there are so few. Partly this relates, one may presume, to the black hole of the two world wars, which sucked in the more considered attempts at international exchange. Yet it also owes much to the fact that the comparative impulse came to express itself, in this period, in a number of alternative terms: avant-garde, international, European. Foremost among these terms was the notion of 'crisis'.

If the years 1914–45 represent the darkest period of modern European history, they also mark its most sustained period of conceptualization. This is not, in fact, a paradox: the sense of crisis that pervades the period produces a heightened sense of urgency, of rushing to save European culture against its own ruin. Last-ditch attempts at asserting a shared cultural legacy abound; despite—or perhaps because of—all evidence to the contrary, 'Europe' is mobilized, time and again, as the common basis for comparison between competing nations. The period from which this emerges most clearly are the years immediately following World War One. In the aftermath of such carnage, the idea of Europe as an overarching category assumed quasi-redemptive status, with figures of the stature of Romain Rolland, Stefan Zweig, and Benedetto Croce asserting its continuing relevance as the cultural precondition for comparison and reconciliation. The period represented the high-water mark, in other words, of attempts to establish what Count Richard von Coudenhove-Kalergi would call, in his manifesto of 1923, *Paneuropa*.

The prodigiously polyglot Coudenhove-Kalergi (1894–1972) was in many ways the founder of the European Union. In the course of a life dedicated to European unification, he fought tirelessly for greater political and cultural collaboration between the various continental countries, advocating a 'United States of Europe'. As the son of an Austro-Hungarian diplomat and a Japanese heiress, his own multinational heritage convinced him of the need for enhanced integration: 'the man of the future will be of mixed race', he wrote, somewhat misguidedly, in 1925. 'Today's races and classes will gradually disappear owing to the vanishing of space, time, and prejudice.' Here as elsewhere, Coudenhove-Kalergi's pan-Europeanism offered an antidote to the bubbling poison of fascism that was starting to corrode Europe.

Polyglot figures of this sort, switching effortlessly between a dizzying array of languages, embody the internationalist spirit behind comparative approaches to literature in the early 20th century. The cultural and intellectual ambition that drives such figures is quite staggering at times, but it also risks reinforcing a lingering sense of Europe as the controlling centre of the world. Europe may be only 'a little promontory on the continent of Asia', wrote the French poet Paul Valéry (1871–1945) in an influential essay of 1919, but it is also 'the brain of a vast body'. Valéry's essay 'The Crisis of the Mind' is perhaps the single most enduring document of the European mentality in this period. First published in English, the essay begins by acknowledging the death drive of Modernity—'We later civilizations . . . we too now know that we are mortal'—before proceeding to adumbrate the crisis of European culture in appropriately elegiac terms. The common cause of contemporary culture, the poet suggests, is its frailty.

From the point of view of comparative literature, Valéry's essay outlines what one might term a graveyard model of comparison.

Like an 'intellectual Hamlet', the modern European meditates on the skulls of fallen giants: Leonardo da Vinci, Kant, Hegel—they all oppress him with their tombstone gravity. One day, Valéry asserts, even the names France, England, and Russia may sound to future ears like Nineveh and Babylon do to ours, ghostly echoes of a distant past. The three enduring legacies that underlie the European mind—the Roman, the Christian, and the Greek—have driven the continent for thousands of years, but they are also what risks disappearing now that Europe looks like disintegrating. The military crisis may have passed, but economic crisis determines the present—and who knows how our intellectual crisis will dictate the future? At stake for cultural critics of the 1920s and 1930s was nothing less than the existence of European culture.

Of course, critics did not always agree on how best to serve this culture. Broadly speaking, one can divide approaches to comparative literature in this period into left-wing and right-wing methodologies, into progressive and conservative visions of the European literary legacy. The left-wing vision emerged principally from Eastern Europe, with its socialist arguments about the precise relationship between aesthetics and politics. Thinkers as disparate as the Russian and Czech formalists on the one hand, and genre theorists such as Georg Lukács or Mikhail Bakhtin on the other, all saw themselves as perpetuating, in their differing ways, the Marxist legacy of politically engaged criticism.

The debates between Lukács and Bertolt Brecht regarding the European tradition brought these differences to a head. In a version of comparative literature by another name, over the course of the 1930s Lukács and Brecht disputed the extent to which pre-Marxist literature—from the Greeks to the Renaissance, from Shakespeare to the Romantics—retained continuing relevance for the modern age. With the 'social mission' of art as the prize—and drawing on an extraordinarily broad range of reference, from English opera to Japanese Noh plays (to take just Brecht)—the two intellectual pugilists pursued a kind of Marxist quarrel of the ancients and moderns: in the red corner, the new aesthetics of committed literature; in the blue corner, the bourgeois Humanist inheritance. This was comparative literature with added ideological punch.

It wasn't only the left-wing critics who came out swinging, however. If many of the leading modernists came to hold conservative views, this was also true of the comparatists. Oswald Spengler's bestseller *The Decline of the West* (1918–22) set the tone for many a postwar jeremiad about the passing of the 'European mind'. Spengler's broad-brush approach to history, culture, and religion was nothing if not comparative; not only his tone, but also his methodology influenced authors of the stature of T.S. Eliot and Gottfried Benn. Yet equally there were subtler, less strident ways of seeking to 'conserve' the European legacy—and it was at this point that a golden generation of comparatists came to the fore.

Stamboul training

It is one of the more mordant ironies of modern intellectual history that the Nazi fetishization of 'national' culture should have given such decisive impetus to the development of international modes of criticism. The increasingly autocratic tenor of the 1930s led a generation of comparatists to take refuge in the international republic of letters; for German—and above all, for German-Jewish—cultural critics, comparative modes of thinking began to assume decisive, existential importance. Pushed into exile at first metaphorically, and then literally, such critics consoled themselves by taking the long view of European culture. Try as he might, Hitler could not efface history.

Following the cessation of hostilities in 1918, an ambitious group of German-language scholars had started turning their attention abroad. In the spirit of postwar reconciliation, these scholars of *Romanistik*—a discipline that is by definition comparative, working across Romance languages such as French, Spanish, and

Italian—adopted a consciously European mindset, emphasizing overarching categories such as Romance or Latin literatures as a way of resisting what they perceived as the narrow reductionism of national traditions. If the work of these critics represents the last great hurrah of the European model of comparative literature, it is because they had already gone into a kind of voluntary intellectual exile before some of them were forced into a compulsory geographical one. Among the various influential comparatists of this period—other significant figures in which included the Hungarian scholars Mihály Babits and Antal Szerb, who respectively wrote histories of 'European' (1935) and 'World' literature (1941) marked by the collapse of the Austro-Hungarian empire in 1918—three great names stand out: Ernst Robert Curtius (1886–1956), Leo Spitzer (1887–1960), and Erich Auerbach (1892–1957).

Often grouped together as a 'golden age' of comparative literature, the three critics in fact displayed considerable differences of talent and temperament. A deeply conservative figure, Curtius enjoyed the most conventional career of the three, obtaining a post in Bonn around the start of World War One and staying there throughout World War Two. Sometimes suspected, for this very reason, of implicit collaboration with the Nazi regime, Curtius in fact cast his net as widely as possible across the Humanist history of European culture, promoting Franco-German understanding and turning in particular to what he saw as the neglected pre-modern period. Throughout the years of the Third Reich, Curtius was working on what would emerge, in 1948, as one of the enduring masterpieces of the discipline: *European Literature and the Latin Middle Ages*.

The importance of Curtius's study can be measured not only by its geographical breadth, but also by its historical depth. Ranging from Antiquity to Modernity, from Homer to Goethe, Curtius traces the 'Europeanization' of literary history, focusing in particular on medieval literature in Latin as a pivotal period in which the presence of a *lingua franca* enabled modern European culture to emerge. In this, his approach was typical of the age: alongside a defiant insistence on international exchange, much of the best work of the 1940s is characterized by a return to the always already comparative Middle Ages. In a letter of 1944, Curtius outlined the appeal of the period in memorably pragmatic terms: 'It doesn't seem to have dawned on anyone how nonsensical the modern division of labour is between national languages, national literatures, and national philologies. What would one think of a medieval historian who only wrote about German events and who only made use of German-language sources?'

Curtius's historical approach to comparative literature can be set against the philological methodology favoured by Spitzer. The most mercurial of the three great *Romanisten*, the Viennese Spitzer was a polyglot in the best central European tradition. Ranging with equal facility over numerous languages, Spitzer was the comparatist's comparatist, combining philological and psychological analysis to incisive effect. Underpinning his prolific output was a recurring preoccupation with stylistics, with the ways in which linguistic detail reflects conceptual argument. Style, in Spitzer's hands, emerged as something like the body language of language, offering vital clues to its movements and meaning.

By the time of his essays on *Linguistics and Literary History*, published in the same year as Curtius's masterpiece in 1948, Spitzer had come to summarize his methodology under the concept of the 'philological circle'. In a manner typical of his approach to stylistics, Spitzer held that a single stylistic feature—Rabelais's use of neologisms, for instance—could be used to open up a broader understanding of a work as a whole; this whole then modifies and contextualizes, in turn, our view of the stylistic features. Something similar could be said to apply to Spitzer's view of the European tradition more generally: analysis of a single text opens up its linguistic details; but these details are then understood within the broader, comparative context of what the Germans term *Geistesgeschichte* (intellectual history), a context that alters, in turn, our perception of the individual work. Spitzer would no doubt have endorsed Nabokov's memorable advice to his students to 'fondle the details'.

It is striking, however, that there is one major context that these Romanists largely ignored, namely the biographical. The omission is all the more telling given their own circumstances: the decision to focus on the philological legacy of the Humanist tradition can be seen as an attempt to distance themselves from the swirling chaos of their times. In the cases of Spitzer and Auerbach, this metaphorical distance became literal as they fled into exile. In the fateful year of 1933, Spitzer left Nazi Germany for a position in Istanbul; three years later, he left Europe for a Chair at Johns Hopkins University in Baltimore. Auerbach would inherit Spitzer's position in Istanbul, fleeing Germany, for his part, in 1935. For a few short years, then, Istanbul became the training ground for comparative literature as it would emerge after the war.

The postwar development of the discipline arguably owes more to Erich Auerbach than to any other single thinker. Partly this is attributable to the glamour of exile: for a discipline as susceptible to symbolic capital as comparative literature, Auerbach's association with the city on the Bosphorus—poised between East and West, between Asia and Europe—is hard to resist. It is also, however, a function of his extraordinarily wide-ranging work, above all his masterpiece *Mimesis: The Representation of Reality in Western Literature* (1946). Written during the war years in Istanbul—Auerbach would move to the USA in 1947—*Mimesis* set the template for comparative literature in the second half of the 20th century. In a series of close readings ranging from Homer to Virginia Woolf, Auerbach extrapolates from what he terms 'points of departure' to recount the history of Western literature as a constant renegotiation between high and low styles, and between differing levels of realism. In the opening chapter, to take just one example, he contrasts the moment in which the former nursemaid

8. 'Odysseus and Eurycleia', Christian Gottlob Heyne.

Eurycleia recognizes the homecoming hero Odysseus by his scar (see Figure 8) with Abraham's sacrifice of Isaac in the Book of Genesis, before opening out into a broader discussion of modes of description in the *Odyssey* and the *Old Testament* more generally. Having established this comparative technique, Auerbach then pursues it all the way through the classical, medieval, and Modern periods.

Remarkably, Auerbach claimed that he did all this without reference to 'a rich and specialized library', stranded as he was in wartime Istanbul. This legend of the bookless, isolated scholar is no doubt overstated, but it is no less instructive for that. Some have even argued that it is the reason for the book's success, suggesting that Auerbach was forced to write a more original book than he might otherwise have done had he clung more slavishly to his sources. Yet his respect for the Western tradition is obvious, and for all its originality *Mimesis* is a conservative book in the best sense of the term, an attempt to conserve Humanist culture in the era of Auschwitz. The elegiac tone that this produces is part of its power: the great age of these major Germanic comparatists, working in heroic exile from the Nazis, was also the *late* age of European culture as defined by its distance from its Latinate, Christian roots. If Auerbach remains such a pivotal figure in the history of the discipline, it is because he both celebrated the past and anticipated the future.

Nowhere is this more evident than in an essay of 1952 entitled 'Philology of World Literature'. Auerbach acknowledges that the move beyond Europe is starting to gain purchase by this point, but he also shrewdly identifies the problem with *Weltliteratur* as it is developing in these postwar years: with the rapid spread of only two dominant models of culture—European-American and Russian-Bolshevik—differences in language and literature risk being flattened out and standardized, such that the dream of world literature may soon be 'at once realized and destroyed'. Auerbach's own experience of exile echoes into his plangent description of what one might term, with reference to Spitzer's philological circle, the 'comparative circle': the most valuable asset a critic has is his own culture—yet it is only when he moves away from this culture that he acquires true insight into it. By the end of World War Two, the same logic might be said to apply to Europe.

'Comp lit' goes global

In the footsteps of pioneering figures such as Spitzer and Auerbach, the discipline of comparative literature began gathering pace in the 1950s largely as a transatlantic affair. If Hitler helped develop the nuclear bomb in America by driving his Jewish scientists away from Europe, he did something similar with literary criticism. European émigrés took their expertise to the

East Coast universities, and their influence continued into the next generation of leading comparatists such as George Steiner or Jean Starobinski, Europeans with (at least partly) American training. Comparative literature had outgrown its continental origins.

Perhaps the most influential figure in the development of what soon came to be known as 'comp lit', in the USA, was René Wellek (1903–95). A Czech émigré at Yale, Wellek wrote numerous important literary studies, including *Theory of Literature* (co-authored with Austin Warren in 1949) and the eight-volume *A History of Modern Criticism*. His doctrine was the broadest of churches; rejecting the narrower, largely French focus on sources and influences, Wellek understood 'comparative' as indicating any approach 'transcending the limits of one national literature'. Ideally, he argued in an essay entitled 'The Crisis of Comparative Literature' (1959), one would simply do away with the adjective altogether, speaking of 'professors of literature' just as one does of professors of philosophy. Wellek's inclusive understanding of the discipline helped found what is sometimes known as the 'American School' of comparative literature, a theoretically inclined version of the discipline that is still thriving today.

That is not to say that he necessarily agreed with such theoretical developments. Wellek in fact came to criticize what he termed the 'new nihilism' of deconstruction and poststructuralism, concerned that its linguistic self-obsession would scare off students and deprive literature of its basic Humanist resonance. Whether this emphasis on rhetorical technicalities antagonized students or attracted them—certain kinds of graduate students will always be drawn to difficulty—there is no doubt that the comparative curriculum in the USA became increasingly theoretical, with figures like the 'Yale School' critics Geoffrey Hartman and Paul de Man advocating critical theory as an essential element of the discipline in the 1960s and 1970s. 'The emphasis', de Man wrote in one curriculum proposal of 1975, 'has increasingly moved toward literature as a language about language, or a metalinguistic discipline'. Given that Wellek himself never learned to speak this meta-language, it is ironic that so many of its native speakers should have given the prestigious lecture series in comparative literature named after him at the University of California.

Beyond the USA, the discipline began establishing itself worldwide in the postwar period. Broadly speaking, comparative literature evolved over the second half of the 20th century as an enduring reaction against the nationalist fervour of the first half. Jewish literary scholars took their 'European mind' with them as they fled the continent, but they also took with them a sense of being irrevocably unhoused, a kind of transcendental homelessness, to borrow a phrase from Lukács. The comparative perspective emerged as a means of making cultural virtue out of political necessity, as a way of establishing a permanent state of exile in the spaces between cultures. It is no surprise, then, that smugglers and spies should have become the metaphors of choice for comparatists—'lifelong, I have tried to act as a double or triple agent', writes Steiner in his autobiography, 'seeking to suggest to one great language and literature the necessary presence of the other'. It is equally unsurprising that many of the most original developments in the discipline should have emerged from the global margins.

The realignment of comparative literature as a global discipline—with its attendant reassessment of the language of 'centre' and 'peripheries'—began to take hold in earnest in the 1960s. Indian, Chinese, and African versions of the discipline had long existed, all with their own local emphases and inflections (the first department of comparative literature was opened in India in 1956, for instance), but they had struggled to gain attention in a literary marketplace dominated by the major Western languages. By the time of the social upheavals of the 1960s, however, established power structures and authorities were increasingly coming under fire, culturally as well as politically. The long march of postcolonialism through the intellectual institutions of the West began to gather pace after the Caribbean theorist Frantz Fanon published *The Wretched of the Earth* in 1961, and the subsequent student movements shared the sense of rising up in international solidarity against national strictures. The literary—and in particular, 'French'—theory that would come to shape comparative literary studies throughout the 1970s and 1980s developed out of this spirit of globalized thinking. It has often been noted that many of the leading thinkers of this period—Jacques Derrida with his doctrine of deconstruction, Julia Kristeva with her concept of 'intertextuality' (see Box 6)—emerged not from literary centres such as Paris, but from the cultural peripheries of Algeria or Bulgaria. In a famous phrase of the time, the empire was writing back.

Box 6 Intertextuality

First introduced by the Bulgarian-French critic Julia Kristeva in 1966, the term 'intertextuality' has enjoyed an astonishingly successful career across the Humanities. All texts, the original idea suggests, are constructed through 'the absorption and transformation' of other texts; every piece of writing is 'a mosaic of quotations'. Although this was almost literally true of modernist works such as *The Waste Land* or *Finnegans Wake*—with their mixture of allusion, quotation, pastiche, and translation—in the multimedia era of saturated knowledge intertextuality has developed into a more diffuse, metaphorical term encompassing any kind of reference by one text to another. As a model for comparative literature, intertextuality offers a significantly broader canvas than 'influence', since it highlights not only the relationship of one work to another, but also the ways in which we make sense of this relationship through pre-existing frameworks. Meaning itself, in short, is to be found in the spaces 'between' texts.

It is still writing back. The theories and debates that defined comparative literature as the 20th century drew to a close—translation studies, cultural studies, cosmopolitanism, feminism, Orientalism—remain with us today, albeit in altered form. They do not constitute the history so much as the continuing story of the discipline; as such, their proper place is in Chapter 4 of this book. Comparative literature has long since become a global enterprise (albeit one that has increasingly sought to question the very idea of globalization), and its present state reflects its—constantly contested—position as a literary United Nations. However problematic the historical emphasis on Europe remains, it has driven the discipline's development as lubricant, irritant, and secret agent of international relations. If comparative literature has become ever more politicized over the course of its history, it is only by understanding this history that its present state—and possible future status—can be fully appreciated.

Chapter 4
Disciplines and debates

Writing in 1993, the British scholar Susan Bassnett claimed that comparative literature was in decline; ten years later, the Indian critic Gayatri Chakravorty Spivak went one step further and declared the 'Death of a Discipline'. Barely a decade on, such obituaries have been proven emphatically wrong. Arguably more than any other discipline in the Humanities, comparative literature has experienced a surge of interest in recent years, driven by its strategic position between languages, literary criticism, and cultural studies. Indeed, it is in many ways defined by this position, by its porous relationship to neighbouring areas of scholarship; equal parts parasite and chameleon, comparative literature draws sustenance from other fields of enquiry just as it takes on their colours. If this makes it particularly vulnerable to changes in intellectual fashion—itself an important, if underexplored subject—it also makes it a placeholder for broader debates about the changing status and purpose of literary culture in the 21st century.

The very term 'comparative literature' is in many ways a category in search of a meaning. Perhaps the biggest lesson of recent years is that both parts of it are provisional. We have seen how the adjective 'comparative' alters its emphasis with changing political and linguistic circumstances; yet the noun 'literature', too, is far from the stable signifier of traditional assumption. With the rise of literary theory in the 1970s, and of cultural studies in the 1980s, the idea of the 'text' began to be contested. As the barriers between 'high' and 'popular' culture became increasingly blurred, as the concept of the 'canon' became increasingly problematic, the previously unquestioned legitimacy of literature as the ultimate form of verbal art came under fire. *Comparative* literature, already inherently contingent, was doubly destabilized. Now more than ever, it asserted itself as an *in*discipline.

Another way of saying this is that since the 1960s comparative literature has splintered into a range of competing disciplines. Perhaps the most accurate way to gauge its place within the Humanities today is thus to consider its various incarnations in neighbouring disciplines, including literary theory, cultural studies, postcolonialism, world literature, translation studies, and reception studies. Understood as a composite of these and other related fields, comparative literature always presupposes a *point* of comparison; in this sense, comparative practices are always also comparative prejudices (even if, following the argument of the philosopher Hans-Georg Gadamer, prejudices are not necessarily negative, since they make judgements possible in the first place). Given the emphasis that it places on the critic as well as on the creator, the indiscipline of comparative literature emerges from these debates as a mode of enquiry in which the observer's predilections—and presuppositions—are as important as those of the object under observation. Comparative literature is also, in short, comparatists' literature.

Literary theory

At the heart of contemporary conceptions of comparative literature is a paradox. In order to justify itself, it has become ever more theoretical; yet for this reason the ostensible object of this theory—literature—has become ever more marginalized. Theoretical discussions of the subject have proliferated, to such an extent that they sometimes seem to push out the actual work of comparing one text with another; within the academy, comparison is often more conceptualized than carried out, more theorized than practised. It is impossible to understand the growth of comparative literature, in short, without also understanding the growth of literary theory.

The astonishing success of literary theory across a broad range of the Humanities—as exemplified by such influential schools as structuralism, poststructuralism, feminism, and postcolonialism—has depended on necessarily comparative premises. Literary theory emerged, that is to say, out of comparative literature: its iconoclastic energy derives, among other sources, from a rejection of neat, national traditions, from an attempt to rethink traditional models of writing. Theory, unlike practice, travels readily between countries; in the international marketplace of ideas, theoretical models are easy to transfer, since they are, 'in theory', universally applicable. That this encourages a natural tendency for ambitious comparatists to theorize about their subject is hardly a surprise. Writing *about* comparing has always been as central to the discipline as comparing writing.

What has changed in the last fifty years is that literary theory has emerged as a discipline in its own right. If comparative literature was a key battlefield for the 'theory wars' of the 1970s and 1980s (see Box 7), its landscape bears the scars, perhaps the most significant of which is that the very concept of 'literature' became problematic. In his seminal *Course in General Linguistics* (first published posthumously in 1916), the Swiss thinker Ferdinand de Saussure had proposed a basic distinction between language understood as a collective phenomenon (*langue*) and speech understood as an individual intervention (*parole*). In calling attention to the social and linguistic codes implicit in how we understand 'works' of literature—to what one might term the relationship between text and context—Saussure's distinction effectively marked the starting point of modern literary theory.

Box 7 Theory wars

Modern literary theory—the roots of which go back to Saussure's linguistics at the start of the 20th century, and to the Romantics a century before him—took off in the 1960s. As higher education expanded in the postwar decades, scholars in the Humanities began focusing less on texts themselves and more on the 'structures' of language, and on the ways in which we write about (and indeed how we write about how we write about) texts: criticism became 'theory'. Throughout the 1970s and 1980s, so-called theory wars raged between opposing ideologies: structuralists decried Marxists, feminists attacked Freudians. However self-involved such spats may now seem—at times they recall Monty Python's People's Front of Judea squabbling with the Judean People's Front—at stake in such debates was an essentially political question: who has the right to say what literature means? Theorizing literature meant politicizing literature, whether understood as a local or a universal phenomenon.

This increased self-consciousness regarding the preconditions of writing had important consequences for comparative literature, placing an ever-greater premium on the ideological allegiances of the critic. Literary theory has had the paradoxical effect of constraining the autonomy of literature, depicting it as a product of the forces—economic, psychological, political, cultural, or sexual—acting upon it. *Hamlet*, seen through psychoanalytic eyes, emerges as a story of Oedipal conflicts; *The Tempest*, reread from a postcolonial perspective, reflects the early modern exploitation of the New World. The critic's role becomes to tease out what the text 'really' means, what it tells us despite its ostensible intentions; the comparative critic's role, by extension, becomes to compare what numerous texts really mean, and to establish what literature understood as an interlinguistic phenomenon tells us despite its ostensible intentions.

All of which raises the basic question of what the 'literary' really is. As René Wellek noted in 1959, 'we must face the problem of "literariness", the central issue of aesthetics'; translated into the terms of high theory (sometimes termed 'French theory'), Wellek's literariness re-emerges as Roland Barthes's *écriture*. From his first book, *Writing Degree Zero* (1953), through to later works such as *The Pleasure of the Text* (1973), Barthes developed an original perspective on the ways in which textual meaning is produced as 'writing'. Importantly from the point of view of comparative literature, Barthes effectively weaponizes literary style as an ideological phenomenon: in *Writing Degree Zero*, for instance, he opposes individual style to collective language (Saussure's *langue*), praising Albert Camus's *The Outsider* as an example of 'white writing' that resists, through its neutrality, ideological appropriation (unlike, say, 19th-century realism with its self-conscious claims to the status of 'Art'). To compare styles is thus to compare ideologies.

Barthes's notion of *écriture* was given a decisive twist in 1967, the year in which Jacques Derrida published three major books. Derrida's aim, famously, was to 'deconstruct' the Western tradition; the main way that he set out to achieve this was by picking apart the standard binary oppositions—presence vs. absence, speech vs. writing, nature vs. culture—that structured Western thought. Derrida's principal weapon in this undertaking was his notion of *différance*, a term that he coined to signify how meaning is produced through a simultaneous process of differing and deferring that renders that meaning at once plural and never quite present. Quite aside from the inherently comparative nature of Derrida's approach—he took his texts from a range of linguistic traditions—his startlingly incisive methodology had two major implications for comparative literature. First, the concept of *différance* entails a comparative approach to language itself: meaning only emerges in the interstices and 'differences' between one sign and another (for instance, between *différence* and *différance*). Second, the project of deconstruction could be—and was—extended to the relationship between national traditions, such that the 'canon' of Western literature itself began to be picked apart and re-examined. In an anti-authoritarian era, the consequences of Derrida's attack on the ideological premises of language were far-reaching.

One of these consequences was the rise of theoretically inflected feminism. The field of 'women's writing' (*écriture féminine*) was equally ripe for deconstruction, its premises and technique dictated for so long by patriarchal presuppositions. Over the course of the 1970s, theorists such as Hélène Cixous and Julia Kristeva came to focus on 'the madwoman in the attic'—the title of an influential reconsideration of Victorian literature by Sandra Gilbert and Susan Gubar—exploring how female writers struggled to develop their own voices under pressure from male conceptions of language and authorship (what became known as 'phallocentrism'). The laugh of the Medusa, to cite Cixous's influential essay of 1975, became a rallying cry for the feminist reconceptualization of approaches to literature, and emerged as a basis for reassessing the hierarchy of major and minor—understood as masculine and feminine—texts. To compare literatures was also, under this new dispensation, to compare the genders of literatures; the madwoman in the attic gave way to the comparatist in the cellar, laying the foundations for a gender-specific reading of literary tradition.

The rise of literary theory thus signalled a renewed attention to the rhetorical techniques of literature, as well as to the very concept of literature understood as a cultural construct. In truth there is no such thing as 'theory', only a proliferation of theories, each one foregrounding a particular *method*—from structuralism to deconstruction, from psychoanalysis to feminism—rather than a given *topic* (to return to the terms discussed in Chapter 2). But the underlying consequence for comparative literature is clear: namely, an increased self-consciousness regarding the notions of both 'comparison' and the 'literary'. If comparative literature remains a highly theoretical discipline, it is because of this basic tendency to question and contest its own premises.

Cultural studies

As literary theory was beginning to take hold in Paris in the 1950s and 1960s, on the other side of the Channel a different kind of intellectual movement was developing. With the increasingly mixed, postcolonial society of the postwar era came an increasingly broad, postmodern sense of culture. Previously taken to indicate the elite achievements of the human mind, the term now started to include within its purview a much wider range of reference, from minority sub-cultures to majority consumerism. Where literary theory engages almost exclusively with extremely complex works of art—Derrida's *Dissemination* (1972), for instance, discusses text such as Mallarmé's *A Throw of the Dice* or Philippe Sollers's *Numbers*—the new science was to be a much broader church, eclectic in its interests and ecumenical in its endeavours. In the spirit of postwar democratization, the undereducated as well as the overeducated were now afforded equal legitimacy in their customs and habits, the mandarins and the masses viewed as part of the same social fabric. With this panoramic perspective, a new discipline was born: *cultural studies*.

The study of culture, to take just the English-speaking world, goes back at least as far as major conservative thinkers such as Matthew Arnold in the 19th century and T.S. Eliot in the early 20th, with the former's *Culture and Anarchy* published in 1869 and the latter's *Notes Towards the Definition of Culture* in 1948. Cultural studies, however, was very much a postwar invention. Where the study of culture took as its focus a traditional understanding of 'high' art, cultural studies turned the idea on its head. As developed by pioneering figures such as Richard Hoggart and Stuart Hall—both associated with the Birmingham School—cultural studies was as much a sociological as an aesthetic theory. Hoggart's *The Uses of Literacy* (1957), echoed and expanded by like-minded thinkers including

Raymond Williams and E.P. Thompson, advocated the continuing vitality of working-class culture, in part as a means of resisting the increasing hegemony of what their German colleagues in the Frankfurt School would call the (largely American) 'culture industry'. Hall, a 'cultural comparativist' formed by his experiences growing up as a colonial subject in Jamaica, was equally at home discussing Henry James as a 'diasporic' novelist or the politics of race, class consciousness or contemporary cinema. For this postwar generation of critics, culture was to be found in the grass roots as much as in the Hollywood hills.

If both the Birmingham and the Frankfurt schools tended to left-wing, not to say Marxist analyses of prevailing orthodoxies and power structures, there were also important differences between them. Unlike their German counterparts, for instance, the British cultural theorists—whose tactics Hall pithily defined as 'talking culturally about politics and politically about culture'—were particularly interested in youth culture as an expression of identity and class-consciousness, as well as in the politics of immigrant and minority cultures such as those of West Indians or East Asians. Perhaps the defining difference between the two approaches, however, was the interest that the British cultural theorists developed not only in advanced art, but also in everyday artefacts: newspapers, cinema, television, advertisements. In the postwar era of flattened cultural hierarchies, a text could be anything designated as such; it is the way that we perceive the text that assigns it this status, not its inherent qualities. Textuality, it emerged, is in the eye of the beholder.

The implications for comparative literature were obvious. In the age of mass media, two basic courses were now available to the comparatist: either to cling to the 'canon' as the only legitimate source of culture; or to embrace the brave new world of the textual revolution. Roland Barthes's *Mythologies* (1957) provides an early expression of the rapidly blurring lines between the two courses.

Presented as a study of 'semiology' or the science of signs, the book is in many ways a primer in media studies as it was developing in the 1950s, suggesting the ways in which 'theory' and 'culture' were emerging as mutually informing concepts. Modernity, like Antiquity, has its mythologies, and Barthes's eagle eye finds them harnessed in the service of capitalism in the most improbable of places: wrestling, soap advertisements, Einstein's brain. In one essay, he decodes a photograph of a black boy in uniform saluting on the cover of *Paris Match* (see Figure 9) as a collection of signifiers intended to show that 'France is a great empire', capable of eliciting the devotion of all its citizens irrespective of race or colour.

We are all, Barthes thereby implies, complicit in the great brainwashing of the modern era, duped by big business and greedy government. With considerable ingenuity, he exposes the work of culture in the age of ideological manipulation, astutely identifying the ways in which linguistic signs signal more than they mean to.

What Barthes's seminal study also shows, however, is that the role of the critic was becoming increasingly politicized. Barthes adopts a pose that would become common over the next fifty years, namely that of high culture appropriating low culture. By taking the mass media seriously, while at the same time exposing its manipulative mechanisms, the critic is able to show not only that he lives in his era, but also that he is wise to its tricks. Cunningly, Barthes thereby implies his own, meta-mythological narrative: the goody is the critic, an intellectual superman with X-ray vision who can see through the ideological surfaces of contemporary culture; the baddy is the bourgeoisie, that recurring villain of the French intelligentsia, wedded to the false consciousness of consumerism. In effect, then, such an approach—one anticipated by an earlier generation of thinkers such as Walter Benjamin or Theodor Adorno—replaces one mythology with another, that of the critical hero undaunted by the overwhelming forces ranged against him.

9. 'A comparative order of facts, ideas, decisions': colonialism in a glossy magazine. Reproduced from Roland Barthes, *Mythologies* (1957).

This sleight-of-hand helps to explain the success of both literary theory and cultural studies as models of comparative literature. Both approaches—whether to elite art or to mass-market media—foreground the critic, raising his work from its traditional, secondary role to the status of a primary intervention in contemporary culture. The interpretive power of cultural studies, to be sure, is considerable: with its combination of aesthetics and sociology, and its focus on urgent contemporary issues, it represents a genuinely comparative undertaking, interdisciplinary *avant la lettre* in its gay science of mixed media and collapsed hierarchies. Yet it also places a particular burden of responsibility on the critic, who must now not merely analyse pre-existing texts—whether verbal, like literature, or visual, like skin colour—but also identify and politicize them. To adapt Marx: literary critics have only interpreted the world; the point, for cultural critics, is to see through it.

No longer beholden, then, to an already established set of canonical works, the cultural critic is given free licence to compare whatever catches her attention; it is the very act of analysis and comparison that dignifies the chosen artefacts with the status of 'text'. Whether the same level of subtlety and sophistication is present in an advertisement as in a poem or novel is irrelevant; it is the critic who brings this apparatus with her. The advent of cultural studies has thus simultaneously lowered and raised the stakes for comparative literature: lowered, because *everything* is now subject to comparison, not just 'literary' texts; raised, because the choice of texts to be compared inevitably implies a political position. Here more than ever, comparison emerges as an ideological as well as an aesthetic enterprise.

Postcolonialism

Nowhere is this ideological undertone more evident than in the context of postcolonial theory. Perhaps the single most influential theory to have emerged in the last fifty years, postcolonialism developed following the dissolution of the major European empires after World War Two. The British in Asia and the French in Africa provide the two most obvious examples of continents in which retreating powers left behind a contested cultural legacy, but elsewhere across the world, too—in Latin America, in the

Caribbean—imperial influences continued to be felt and fought. Independence, for many former colonies, was just the beginning.

The implications of postcolonialism for comparative literature are complex and controversial, but the principal issue at stake, in culture as in politics, is that of power. Who controls the production and interpretation of culture? Who determines the dominant modes of expression? The classic problem of postcolonialism is that of autonomy, in the moral and cultural as well as in the political sense. Politically speaking, a nation can become independent overnight; intellectually speaking, it can take generations. The withdrawal of an imperial power leaves behind an uneasy mixture of local custom and colonial mimicry, of defiance and deference—a situation that is compounded, of course, by the simple fact of having to write in an imported language. In order to be heard internationally, some Indian writers turn to English, some African writers to English or French (the fact that still more do not, preferring to write in their own native languages, is an inconvenient truth that complicates the standard critical emphasis on Anglophone and Francophone literature). As many a 'colonial' writer has asserted, the medium inevitably distorts the message, imposing modes of thought and expression that are not always best suited to conveying local experience. The result risks being a chimera, neither native fish nor foreign fowl.

From the point of view of comparative literature such a chimera is, of course, endlessly fascinating. The very in-betweenness of postcolonial culture, its provisional, politicized nature, its mixture of domestic and foreign influences, and its constantly shifting combination of local context and universal resonance: all this is the very essence of comparison. As with literary theory more generally, postcolonialism as applied to literature is inherently comparative, which explains why it has developed into such a powerful wing of the modern discipline—and into a way, to use the historian Dipesh Chakrabarty's term, of 'provincializing

Europe'. It is hardly surprising, then, that many of its best-known concepts reflect this, enacting what one might term the always already comparative nature of postcolonialism.

The wave of independence that swept over Africa in the 1960s—in 1960 alone, some seventeen sub-Saharan countries regained their sovereignty from France, Britain, and Belgium—was made possible by the new world order of the postwar era. Ideologically speaking, however, a groundswell of anti-colonial sentiment had already been building before the war, nowhere more forcefully than in the imperial capital, Paris. In the early 1930s, in the heart of the French establishment, three black students from the colonies—Aimé Césaire from Martinique, Léon-Gontran Damas from French Guiana, and Léopold Senghor from Senegal—coined the concept of *négritude*. As a provocation, as a way of reclaiming their supposedly 'inferior' racial position as a mark of strength, the term was a masterstroke. As a defining concept of the transition from colonialism to postcolonialism, it resonated into the subsequent careers of its three founders: Césaire and Damas represented their countries to the French parliament; Senghor became the founding president of Senegal. Rarely has theory been spoken so successfully to power.

Aesthetically speaking, *négritude* represented an attempt to assert African values against adopted European ones. The problem, of course, was that in an era of colonial control, in which native and imperial aesthetics were inevitably entangled, this was easier said than done. Theorists such as Césaire and Senghor fought hard to establish what they saw as authentically African art—as opposed to its fashionable imitation in *l'art primitif* of early 20th-century Europe—but the ways in which they did so, inevitably, were themselves informed by European as well as by African thought. Nietzsche's celebrated distinction, as elaborated in *The Birth of Tragedy* (1872), between 'Dionysian' and 'Apollonian' art—the former primal and untamed, the latter serene and controlled—emerged, to cite just one example, as an important intertext: African art was to form the organic, Dionysian counterpart to superficial, Apollonian Europe. In practice, however, the two were understood comparatively, the thought of the one informing the aesthetics of the other.

Alongside Africa, the other major continent to develop postcolonial models of literature was Asia. If reducing such vast continents to a handful of concepts is inevitably misleading—after all, India alone has twenty-two official languages—the single most influential concept to emerge out of postcolonial theory criticized precisely this reductivism. Published in 1978, Edward Said's study *Orientalism* (see Box 8) demonstrated the ways in which European literature has imposed a small number of clichés on—what it takes to be—the 'Orient'. The East emerges as the mirror image of the West: exotic, feminized, submissive. It exists only in the mind of the observer, whose supposed knowledge of

Box 8 *Orientalism*

Europeans have always romanticized Asia, but it took a critic of Edward Said's acumen to see that 'western conceptions of the Orient', to cite his book's subtitle, insinuate themselves even into the stylistic and philological presuppositions of literature. The Orient of writers such as Chateaubriand and Nerval, Said claims in the opening statement of his book, is essentially a European invention; the fact of (Middle) Eastern culture may be indisputable, but the fantasy requires external observers to conceive it as the exotic foil to their own, Christian culture. In the manner of Michel Foucault, Said discerns in this Orientalist fantasy the assertion of knowledge as power. In claiming knowledge of the Orient, Europeans implicitly assert their authority over it; in homogenizing it into one indiscriminate mass, they deny it autonomy. As a model of comparative literature, *Orientalism* thus criticizes the very idea of comparison as predicated upon an imbalance of power.

the Orient—based on little more than legend and myth—gives him power over it. It is the incarnation, in short, of the Other.

Said's groundbreaking model was quickly applied beyond the Orient to all areas of colonial interaction. It has certainly not been without its critics (particularly given the way in which Said appropriated the previously neutral descriptor 'Orientalist' as a pejorative): some have found his concept of Orientalism monolithic and self-undoing, others have criticized his readings of Western texts as unfair and inaccurate. The concept has nonetheless been enormously influential, and indeed it has been extended both backwards—as in Srinivas Aravamudan's study of *Enlightenment Orientalism* (2011)—and sideways, to cognate terms such as 'arcticism' in northern Norway. As a Palestinian, Said was acutely aware of the political and cultural sensitivities surrounding the Western image of the Middle East; as a literary critic schooled in the European tradition, he was alive to the ways in which comparing literatures often amounts to condemning one as inferior. Understood in the broadest sense as a critique of how the observer distorts the object—sometimes called the Wizard of Oz effect ('pay no attention to that man behind the curtain')—Orientalism created a school of comparative literature unto itself.

Influential concepts such as *négritude* and Orientalism suggest that beyond the imbalance of power inherent in colonial literature, the trick of much postcolonial literature has been to make a virtue out of its compound necessity. Although the problematic relationship between colonizer and colonized is nothing new in European literature—one need only think of Robinson Crusoe 'educating' Friday in Daniel Defoe's novel of 1719—it assumed new pertinence in the age of globalization and the imperial 'boomerang'. Writing in 1981, for instance, the Caribbean theorist Edouard Glissant proposed 'diversity' as the appropriate ambition for the postcolonial era, encouraging Western literatures to reflect on a 'new relationship with the world, by which they would signal no longer their preeminent place in the Same, but their shared task in the Diverse'. By 1994, the Indian critic Homi Bhabha had repurposed this into his influential concept of 'hybridity', a condition in which the colonial subject mimics the master and thereby gains a transnational perspective on the shifting balance of power between colonizer and colonized. More recently, 'autoexoticism'—the deliberate appropriation of imperialist misrepresentations in order to subvert them, such as the Irish exaggeration of their own marginality and strangeness—has emerged as a further way of foregrounding the productivity of the postcolonial condition. Comparison itself, in short, has developed into a hybrid.

If comparative literature thrives on the pathos of internationalism, however, it is worth noting that postcolonialism is driven largely by *nationalist* rhetoric. To be sure, it is not generally of the crude, far-right kind that disfigured Europe in the 20th century, but is akin rather to Schiller's image of the 'bent twig' (as picked up by Isaiah Berlin) that springs back against an allegedly superior force in assertion of its independence. Both Glissant and Bhabha, for instance, assert the primacy of native writing in these terms: Glissant defines national literature as 'the urgency for each group to name itself'; Bhabha claims that 'increasingly, "national" cultures are being produced from the perspective of disenfranchised minorities'. International models of postcolonialism, in other words, are predicated upon national self-assertion. Such, we have seen, is the history of comparative literature.

World literature

If there is one model of comparison that has come to the fore since the turn of the millennium, it is that of world literature. The term is hardly new, as we saw in the previous chapter: from Wieland and Goethe to Brandes and Posnett, it resonates across the 19th century as the *de facto* object of study for comparative literature.

Throughout this time its horizons remained decidedly European, however, adumbrating a quasi-colonial vision of the world controlled by an imperial centre. It is only with the advent of the 20th century that world literature took a global turn.

Instructive examples of this development can be found at either end of the century in the contribution to debates on world literature of Bengali. In 1907, the poet and polymath Rabindranath Tagore (1861–1941) was invited to give a lecture to the National Council of Education in Calcutta. Tagore insisted on discussing not comparative, but *world* literature: the Bengali term *Vishwa Sahitya*, he contended, does much greater justice to the diversity of the Indian sub-continent, in part because it does not correspond to the foreign, European notion of comparative literature. Tagore rejects what he sees as the problematic Western emphasis on the 'nation', emphasizing rather the dynamic, interdependent nature of literature, which he views not as 'the mere total of works composed by different hands' but as a 'part of man's universal creativity'. Most of us, admonishes Tagore, think of literature in the manner of a 'rustic', parcelling out patches of land piece by piece. To this provincialism he opposes his concept of *Vishwa Sahitya*, understood as the 'universal spirit' manifesting itself through the verbal arts.

Nearly a century later, another Bengali thinker proposed an alternative form of world literature. In her Wellek Lectures on the *Death of a Discipline* (2003), Gayatri Chakravorty Spivak, whose concept of the 'subaltern' helped open up a debate in the 1980s about how best to give voice to minority cultures, outlines what one might term a postcolonial form of world literature: 'planetarity'. The standard models of Anglophone, Francophone literature, etc., can no longer serve in the post-cold-war era, suggests Spivak; what is now required is a version of comparison that takes into account the non-Western traditions of comparative literature, and that thus allows the 'Global South'—which is to say the less developed, poorer countries previously designated by such terms as 'third world'—to speak for itself, in its own languages, rather than via a centralized, metropolitan elite. Spivak's opposition of the planet to the globe recalls Tagore's opposition of 'world' to 'comparative': globalization suggests corporate control and standardization; the planet, on the other hand, is what we inhabit, 'on loan'. She does not cite him, but Spivak seems to echo Tagore's ecological metaphors; in the era of global warming and climate change, we are all interconnected in ways that go well beyond cartographic distinctions. World literature must become planetary literature.

The example of these two Bengali thinkers—and one could add others, such as the writer and critic Buddhadeva Bose or the historian Dipesh Chakrabarty—suggests that world literature has been revivified by expanding beyond its European origins. Chakrabarty's criticism of the 'historicist' approach to world development—in which capitalist Modernity originates in Europe and then spreads inexorably elsewhere—extends even to the construction of time, tethered as 'Eurochronology' is to a Greenwich, rather than to a global meridian. Certainly the evolution of comparative literature can be criticized in these terms, however noble (some of) its expansionist intentions may have been. All too often, the view from elsewhere has been a view from Europe.

Yet there is no reason why a genuinely intercontinental model of world literature should not be possible. India, in fact, serves as a striking counterpart to Europe, composed as it is of a comparable number of languages and sub-cultures. If a comparative approach to Indian literature emerged, in the 1980s, as a sub-field unto itself, one might equally sketch out comparative literatures for almost all the continents. In the postcolonial age, perhaps every continent requires, to paraphrase Virginia Woolf, a comparative literature of its own. The most influential models of world literature in the postwar era, even those that emerged from Europe, have aspired to this multipolar perspective. In numerous studies of Chinese and comparative literature, for instance, the prolific French sinologist René Etiemble (1909–2002) theorized what he called *littérature universelle*, working tirelessly to demonstrate the ways in which Asian and European literature explored common thematic and stylistic concerns. Etiemble's slogans—the Sartrean manifesto 'comparative literature is humanism', the disciplinary self-consciousness captured by his untranslatable book title *Comparaison n'est pas raison* (1963)—not only helped establish the postwar discipline in France, but also skewered the limited vision of the 'world' that continued to characterize much European thought. Building on the legacy of illustrious forebears such as Montesquieu and Voltaire, Etiemble showed how much the Parisians could learn from the Persians.

More recently, this French conception of global literature has been repurposed in sociological terms. Pascale Casanova's influential vision of *The World Republic of Letters* (1999) proposes not world literature, but 'world literary space' as the key term. Literary history and political history, while obviously related, are not the same thing: the wounded pride of one nation—she gives the example of German classical literature 'fighting back' against Napoleonic hegemony—asserts itself culturally where it cannot politically. A constant push-and-pull thus develops, whereby a supposedly 'lesser' literature seeks to establish its own identity by both irritating and imitating the dominant power. In Casanova's sociological terms, national literatures, and national writers, compete with each other for international legitimacy.

It goes without saying, of course, that literary theorists do the same thing. The development of theories of world literature, and indeed of comparative literature more generally, can be understood through exactly the same models that are applied to literature. Universalism, planetarity, republicanism: such metaphors describe both comparison and comparatist, competing for attention with ever more inflated concepts of how world literature *really* works. Even the much-remarked manifesto 'For a world literature in French' (2007), signed by leading authors from Canada, Tunisia, Senegal, the Congo, and France, announced the death of Francophone literature and the birth of *littérature-monde* as a 'Copernican revolution'. Given such metaphysical claims, it is hard to see where the metaphors have left to go.

Perhaps this inflationary logic is why the most influential model to have emerged in recent years emphasizes world literature not as a stable canon of classic works, but as a 'mode of circulation and of reading'. From Gilgamesh to postmodernism, David Damrosch's *What is World Literature?* (2003) pursues the flow of creation, translation, and production into the literary works themselves, arguing that the texts that achieve 'world' status are those that build the process of circulation into their own reflective structure. For Damrosch, a text enters into world literature by a twofold process: 'first, by being read *as* literature; second, by circulating out into a broader world beyond its linguistic and cultural point of origin'. If global intellectual history teaches us that the universality of an idea can be assessed by the degree to which it is adopted in distant contexts, global literary history can apply a similar test to texts. Indeed, a work can move in and out of world literature, depending on how it is read in a given time; the most 'worldly' works, to use Said's term, are those that gain most in translation. Comparative literature, in this sense, is not so much a canon as a currency.

The language of commerce takes us back to the original Goethean conception of world literature, and forward to the major criticism of the term as it has emerged over the last ten years. As early as 1827, Goethe described world literature as 'the market-place where all nations offer their products', and he himself conceived the notion in part as a way of encouraging the international reception of his own work. From its inception, in other words, world literature has been as much a capitalist as a comparative concept, as much about selling books as scrutinizing them. The most widely discussed critical engagement with the term, Emily

Apter's *Against World Literature* (2013), takes this insight as its starting point, arguing that universalizing models of comparison ignore the problem of what the French philosopher Barbara Cassin calls 'untranslatables' (examples of which, as explored in Cassin's *Dictionary of Untranslatables* of 2004, include terms such as *Heimat*, *saudade*, and *pravda*). In resisting translation, such terms also resist the capitalist logic of international standardization; crossing borders, to cite the great comparative cliché, is precisely what they do not do. No one can read all the languages, which means that for better or for worse foreign texts are translated not only into a language, but also into an idiom familiar to the major markets—with all the attendant risks of misunderstanding and homogenization. Here as elsewhere, then, translation remains the dirty little secret of comparative literature.

Translation studies

The issue of translation is at the very heart of comparative literature. There is a limit, after all, to how many languages even the most gifted of linguists can read; the polyglot literary theorist Roman Jakobson, so the saying goes, spoke seventeen languages, but all of them in Russian. However much we urge ourselves to read in the original, translation is a necessary evil for the comparatist. Yet it is also, of course, a force for good, opening up as it does a whole range of practical and conceptual considerations regarding the relationships between national literatures. Translation, to adapt Oscar Wilde, is the sincerest form of flattery, but it is also the closest form of reading. As a model for comparative literature, it functions both as condition and criticism of how we read.

Translation studies took off in the 1970s. While the problem of translation is as old as Cicero and Horace, Saint Jerome and Luther, it had gained curiously little purchase in the world of literary studies. The theoretical, linguistic turn in comparative literature had left the issue of how texts were carried across languages curiously untouched; outside of the technical sphere of linguistics, discussion had barely moved on from the idea that a translation was simply an inferior imitation of an original. From the mid-1970s onwards, however, scholars such as George Steiner and Itamar Evan-Zohar started asking pertinently impertinent questions about the status and preconditions of translation. Why do some cultures translate more than others? Why are some texts more readily 'translatable' than others, and what does this tell us about how they are perceived by both target and source languages? How has the status of translation altered over the centuries? What gets lost in translation—and what, no less importantly, gets found? As provisional answers to these questions began to be proposed, translation emerged not as a transparent window, but as an opaque, culturally specific process.

An obvious starting point for the discipline was to reflect on the most common metaphors for translation, and on the ways in which they have changed over time. Perhaps the most enduring metaphors, in this context, have been those of fidelity/infidelity. Translations have traditionally been judged either by how 'loyal' they are to their source text—with perceived deviations from the original deemed intrusive and disloyal—or by how free they are. These two master metaphors inform, in turn, the two principal models of translation theory, namely 'domestication' and 'foreignization'. The former holds that the source text should be translated as fluently as possible into the target language, almost as though it had been written in this language (the approach to Greek texts taken by Roman poets such as Horace); the latter maintains that the translator's role is to render her own language 'foreign' by reproducing the syntax and meaning of the original source text as closely as possible, even at the expense of conventional linguistic usage (the approach to Greek texts taken by Romantic poets such as Hölderlin). Third ways come and go—the most influential being perhaps the German critic Walter Benjamin's claim, in an 1923 introduction to his versions of Baudelaire, that translation can access an Ur-text hidden between the lines of the original—but the history of translation, and of translation theory, essentially constitutes a continuing oscillation between these two extremes. Not least, of course, because they too are culturally specific, beholden to changing views of the status, symbolism, and—perhaps most importantly—sales figures of translation.

As a model for comparative literature more generally, translation is so resonant precisely because it represents both the precondition of international communication and the process itself. Translation not only *makes possible* comparison—it is also, itself, an *act* of comparison, 'the intertraffique of the minde', to cite Samuel Daniel's poem in praise of Florio's English version of Montaigne (1603). Conceived in its broadest sense, translation calls into question the politics, the aesthetics, and the ethics of literature; every act of translation, every last linguistic choice, represents an intervention in the field of international relations. Living, as we all do, 'after Babel' (see Box 9) we have no option but to communicate through translation; whether this is even possible is the subject of an enduring debate between 'universalists', who hold that everything can be translated, and 'nominalists', who hold that nothing, strictly speaking, can be translated. It is no surprise, then, that some scholars have gone so far as to posit translation studies as the true future of comparative literature, indeed as its successor.

In her 1993 introduction to comparative literature, Susan Bassnett argued that focusing on translation would help recalibrate the discipline in more genuinely global terms, away from the traditional distinction between major and minor literatures and towards a more egalitarian emphasis on international interaction. Her principal model for this was Itamar Evan-Zohar's theory of literature as a 'polysystem'. In an influential essay of 1978, Evan-Zohar argued that the shifting status of translation within this polysystem reflects the shifting status of the target language.

Box 9 *After Babel*

First published in 1975, George Steiner's *After Babel* places 'aspects of language and translation' at the very heart of literary studies. Ferociously learned, effortlessly polyglot, and fiercely uncompromising in his defence of high culture, Steiner is in many ways the natural successor to mid-20th-century European comparatists such as Auerbach and Spitzer. He goes beyond them, however, in his suggestion that *all* forms of expression can be conceived as processes of translation—even those occurring within one language—since linguistic usage is in constant flux. Ranging from Shakespearean monologues to modernist poems—and from sacred to secular texts—Steiner argues that literature is both an act of, and a reflection on, the communication of meaning; driven by the twin engines of similarity and difference, the mechanisms of translation are the mechanisms of comparison. Combining linguistics, literature, philosophy, and the history of ideas, *After Babel* remains the most influential of Steiner's many contributions to comparative literature.

Put briefly, this means that whenever a culture considers itself 'young', 'peripheral', or in 'crisis', it seeks to reinforce its sense of self by turning to translated works from elsewhere; as national self-confidence develops, so this external need for validation fades away. Increased translation, in short, implies increased insecurity.

Whatever criticisms one might make of this model—how does it square, for instance, with the fact that major cultures such as France and Germany translate so much?—what is striking is how quickly such theories date. It is not only translation that reflects changing cultural priorities, in other words, but also translation theory. In the theoretical fever of the 1970s, the language of structuralist 'systems' was in the air, with Claudio Guillén's

Literature as System (1971) one of several precursors to Evan-Zohar's notion of the literary polysystem. Since the turn of the millennium, by contrast, disciplinary discussion has moved on, with translation becoming part of a more politicized understanding of what Franco Moretti calls a 'world literary system', torn between models of close and distant reading, border crossing and border closing. Increasingly, the focus of comparative literature has been not so much on what gets lost in translation as on what gets least in translation, on the 'untranslatable' terms of Barbara Cassin's dictionary that resist reconceptualization in another language. What Lydia Liu has called 'translingual practice'—the contextually specific resonance of words such as the Western 'self' on the one hand and the Confucian *ji* on the other—has emerged as a way of shifting attention away from straightforward claims of equivalence and towards subtler forms of exchange. If the etymology of translation implies 'carrying over', it is precisely that which resists being carried over that is starting to claim the attention of comparatists. That such a development is merely the latest—and certainly not the last—skirmish in the age-old battle between universalists and nominalists underlines the extent to which translation remains both the prerequisite for, and the very practice of, comparative literature.

Reception studies

If translation suggests one mode of carrying over, 'reception' describes another. Translation ferries meaning *between* languages, as it were on a horizontal axis; reception traces meaning *through* languages, on a vertical axis. Translation is of course itself a form of reception—not least because the major works are constantly being retranslated—but its comparative thrust is largely geographical, across languages and cultures; reception, by definition, works historically, drawing attention to what readers and cultures do with translations. Clearly anything, in principle, can be 'received' by a later culture—certain theoretical schools, such as the 'reader response theory' of Wolfgang Iser and Hans

Robert Jauss, make reception the very basis for literary meaning—but the resonance is greatest where the lineage is longest. As such, the reception of Greek, Roman, and Arabic classics provides one of the most enduring models of comparative literature across the centuries, and can stand for the contemporary prominence of reception studies more generally.

Despite its newly fashionable status in the Anglophone world, classical reception studies are as old as Antiquity. Much of Latin literature amounts to an extended reception study of the Greeks; as Horace writes in his *Epistles*, 'conquered Greece conquered its fierce victor and introduced the arts to rustic Latium'. Perhaps more surprisingly, the Greeks themselves looked back to Persian culture, as Edward Said showed in his influential reading of Aeschylus' tragedy *The Persians* as one of the earliest documents of Orientalism. In some ways, then, the whole discipline of classical studies is about reception, looking back as it does across millennia of cultural accretion. The particular contribution of classical *reception* studies, however, is to focus on the ways in which the classical tradition is reactivated in later societies—thus drawing out the changing meanings created by changing contexts—and to reflect on the cultural and theoretical implications of this process. Out of this juxtaposition comes a new, original perspective not only on both the earlier and the later texts, but also on the relationship between these texts and their respective periods.

The richness of this approach for comparative literature is self-evident. Comparatively speaking, it is better to receive than to give, since the later context is enriched by the vestigial presence of the former. In the quarrel of the ancients and moderns, reception critics read the former through the latter, teasing out the ways in which a later text draws on its predecessor. Indeed, in Jonathan Swift's satirical version of the debate—the so-called 'Battle of the Books', published as part of *A Tale of a Tub* in 1704—it is the books themselves that come to life and fight for supremacy (see Figure 10).

10. The Battle of the Books, original woodcut from *A Tale of a Tub* (1704).

That Swift avoids reaching a conclusion in the debate is only prudent. For while the modern text may not be superior to the ancient one, it cannot help but be informed by it—as well, potentially, as by all the ways in which it has previously been received. Focusing on the reception of classical myth in the Victorian period might show us how the 19th-century ideal of masculinity was constructed through reference to Homeric heroes, but it may also retrospectively alter our view of how Homer was received in earlier times. The reception of 'Oriental' epics such as the *Arabian Nights* (first made available to a European audience in Antoine Galland's French translation of 1704), or of the Persian poem the *Shahnameh* (famous in particular for its history of illustrated manuscripts), tells us as much about the changing status of the Orient as it does about the texts themselves. Reception, in this sense, is like using Georg Brandes' telescope to look not only at the stars, but also at the telescope itself.

Another common approach to reception studies is to consider the evolution of genre distinctions such as tragedy or comedy, or of rhetorical modes such as *anagnorisis* (a moment of recognition) or *katabasis* (a trip to the underworld). Such distinctions allow critics to trace how later works have developed or deviated from their classical source while remaining within a shared frame of reference; Nietzsche's *The Birth of Tragedy*, juxtaposing Wagner with Sophocles, is a case in point. To be sure, this should not be taken to imply that reception is a passive state of affairs in which meaning is simply dictated by the past. On the contrary, new meaning is created by new juxtapositions: writing against the backdrop of the Franco-Prussian war of 1871, Nietzsche repurposes Greek tragedy as a constituent element of European Modernity. Creative reception of this sort can even work its way back to where it started: Edward Fitzgerald's *Rubaiyat of Omar Khayyám* (first published in 1859) essentially reinvented the medieval Persian poet Khayyám not just for modern European, but also for modern Persian readers. Understood in this fashion, reception becomes ‘circulation’, tracking recurring characters in changing contexts—Orpheus in modern poetry, Odysseus in modern cinema—or following processes of cultural transfer across continents. Tradition itself, to borrow Hobsbawm and Ranger’s celebrated term, emerges not just as received but also as ‘invented’.

Yet this idea of ‘tradition’ has, in turn, its own tradition. One of the key contributions of comparative literature understood as reception studies has been to reflect on the ways in which cultural tradition is created, curated, and corralled, on how it is appropriated in support of a prevailing ideology. The idea of the ‘canon’, it has become ever clearer, is never ideologically neutral; certain texts, characters, or even cultures—the ‘tyranny of Greece’ over 19th-century Germany, the Roman obsession of Mussolini’s Italy—are foregrounded at certain times. More generally, intellectual history suggests that there are two main models for understanding tradition: either as an unbroken ‘chain’ of influence, in which every iteration of a motif or myth adds to its cumulative depth (as in our understanding of the ‘tragic’, for instance), or as a series of discrete, elective moments, in which one writer or period selectively evokes another, often very distant period (Keats’s ‘wild surmise’ on first reading Chapman’s translation of Homer). The very idea of reception, in short, has been received in different ways at different times.

Why, then, has it risen to prominence in the 21st century? Part of the answer is simple expediency. Facing an ever-greater struggle to justify its existence, Classics has turned to reception studies as a way of asserting its continuing relevance and self-awareness: Antiquity as a guide to Modernity. More broadly, however, the study of reception has emerged as part of a general turn to forms of history—book history, intellectual history—that prioritize cultural context over semantic content. This historical turn has brought with it a broadening of the comparative perspective, predicated not only on seeing reception as a form of comparison, but also on viewing comparison as a form of reception. Studying the ways culture is received amounts, in the final analysis, to comparing disciplines; that classical reception—or indeed reception studies of any kind—is inherently interdisciplinary suggests its potential for the *in*disciplinary compass of comparative literature, flickering uncertainly between ancient and modern, East and West, North and South. One thing is sure: future debates will add further coordinates. If comparative literature is a compass, it requires constant recalibration.

Chapter 5
The futures of comparative literature

Political education

In 1872, at the tender age of 27, a young professor published his first book. It may now be viewed as a seminal work, but at the time of its publication Nietzsche's *The Birth of Tragedy* was met with deafening silence. The only critic who responded to it was his old school friend Ulrich von Wilamowitz-Moellendorff; in a violent attack, he dismissed Nietzsche's anachronistic approach to criticism as 'philology of the future' (*Zukunftsphilologie*). However seductive the term, it was not intended as a compliment.

Can comparative literature reclaim the insult? For all its past struggles and present debates, comparative literature has an increasingly central role to play in the future of the Humanities. In a world defined by globalization and its discontents, in an academy defined by ever-greater interdisciplinarity, comparison is inescapable. The choice now is not whether to compare, but what and how to compare: books, films, languages, cultures, histories. The philology of the future has become the philology of the present, ranging ever more widely across contemporary culture.

Comparative literature is undoubtedly among the most ambitious of scholarly disciplines. It is also, however, among the most anxious. State-of-the-discipline reports—such as those commissioned at ten-year intervals by the American Comparative Literature Association (ACLA)—regularly betray a sense of unease about the emerging direction of travel. To be sure, comparative literature has long existed in a perpetual state of crisis, and much of its self-conception has accordingly revolved around the rhetoric of mortality and immortality. Metaphors of birth and death (of tragedy, for instance), or of oblivion and renaissance, have characterized comparative literature for centuries, torn as it is between resuscitating the past and revitalizing the present. In recent years, the notion of the 'afterlife' of a work (*Fortleben* in Walter Benjamin's variation of the term, *Nachleben* in that of the art historian Aby Warburg) has become increasingly popular as a way of capturing more creative forms of influence: Shakespeare's afterlives, for instance, form a whole school of comparative literature unto themselves. More broadly, such metaphysical metaphors point to the discipline's obsession with continuity and change, an obsession that reflects its own enduring insecurities regarding its changing status within the Humanities. By tying its fate in this manner to that of established figures and disciplines, comparative literature hopes to ensure its own survival.

This shadow status suggests a paradoxical conclusion: namely, that comparative literature is both central and marginal to literary studies, or perhaps, in what is only seemingly a paradox, central precisely *because* it is marginal. It is central because it draws on almost every discipline in the Humanities, cannily positioning itself in the middle of the Venn diagram of history, politics, languages, and literature; it is marginal because it is not tied to any single tradition, and thus risks being ignored by all of them. The vulnerability of comparative literature, in other words, is both its strength and its weakness. Sensitive as it is to shifting trends, it is also at the mercy of such trends. The risk of a hostile takeover by theoretical jargon, for instance, is a constant threat. A second round of the theory wars would surely be in no one's interest.

More pressing at this point is the *practice* of comparison, and the ways that it pushes at the edges of what we understand as 'literature'. One of the principal developments in recent years has been a move not just towards interdisciplinarity, but also towards transdisciplinarity. 'Inter-art' studies have become ever more prominent: comparison between fiction and films, sculptures and sonnets, figure increasingly on curricula and conferences. 'Transnational', meanwhile, has emerged as a key term within the field, creeping in from neighbouring disciplines such as history and law. Comparative literature, once again, finds itself in the crossfire of the Humanities.

What do such developments tell us about the future of the discipline? Above all, they suggest that both the method of comparison and the object of literature are becoming ever broader in their definitions. There are dangers, as well as opportunities, in such expansionism. Comparing differing media and forms of art can be an extremely fruitful way of opening up new perspectives—on Proust and painting, for instance, or Liszt and literature—but it is not always clear that the particularities of the respective art forms are maintained. 'What is the good of the Arts if they're interchangeable?', asks Margaret Schlegel of her sister Helen's attempts to translate music into painting in E.M. Forster's *Howard's End* (1910), and the question remains pertinent to the contemporary comparatist. Simply extracting content—Proust's references to art, Liszt's use of literary sources—is only of limited interpretive use; much more interesting is to enquire into the formal echoes and exchanges, the ways in which one medium borrows techniques from another. Pursued in this manner, both creator and critic emerge between the arts as comparatists.

'Transnational' interpretations of literature, similarly, are at their strongest when not simply used as a modish synonym for 'comparative'. Taken at its word, the term implies an approach that transcends the structures of nations, implying, to cite just one example, 'a web of social and textual interrelationships linking modernisms worldwide as well as an optic through which to see these links'. While this may seem similar to the traditional understanding of comparison, the difference lies in the attempt to give parity—and thus 'planetarity'—to a range of competing perspectives (the increasingly popular plural 'modernisms' is telling). If the comparative method has long been hostage, as we have seen throughout this book, to the prejudices of the day, imposing comparison on terms that are favourable to the dominant (Western) nation, then transnationalism effectively functions as a warning *against* comparison, against its colonial complicity and tendency to apply national prejudice internationally.

Closely related to this transnational turn is an increasing interest in forms of multilingualism. Historically speaking, comparative literature has tended to reduce regions and continents to one dominant language, dividing up the world according to Francophone, Anglophone, or Hispanophone spheres of influence. Yet areas such as the Maghreb, with its imbrication of dialects and forms of Arabic with French and Spanish, or the Indian sub-continent with its twenty-two official languages, are more accurately understood as multilingual, stubbornly irreducible to the European model of single-language nations. The potential of such a multilingual model of comparison is considerable, since it promises to push comparative literature beyond the increasingly unproductive dichotomy of 'national' and 'foreign', local and colonial languages, as well as to take into account both written and oral texts. It is also, of course, implicitly political as well as cultural, a bottom-up rebuke to top-down monolingualism.

For the sobering reality is that the multilingual are most often the marginal, the disenfranchised on the edges of Western wealth. Understood in literal rather than literary terms, the truly transnational in the 21st century are the refugees and immigrants clustering at border-points, traded back and forth between countries and continents. In a world in which humans are trafficked as ruthlessly as commodities, the metaphors of comparison ring humiliatingly hollow: it is facile to say that words cross borders, when people cannot. Comparative literature will surely have to catch up with this new reality and begin applying itself to the stories of those who are transnational not out of desire, but despair.

Aesthetic education

One way in which it might do this is by conceiving itself, in the terms of the German poet Friedrich Schiller (1759–1805), as a process of 'aesthetic education'. In letters written in the early 1790s in the wake of the French Revolution—around the same time, that is to say, that 'comparative philology' was coming into fashion—Schiller argued that the ideal aesthetic state is one characterized by the Kantian notion of disinterest (defined as the process of engaging with the world selflessly, without vested interest). In such a state, the enlightened, autonomous citizen, finely poised between reason and emotion, sense and sensibility, learns to balance competing intellectual demands through aspiring to an 'ideal of equality'. The aesthetic 'play' of the imagination, freely embraced, creates a safe space for human—and for humanist—self-realization.

That such a state can lead to a process of political and even moral education lies, for Schiller, in the nature of the (truly) aesthetic. It is also what makes it a possible model for the future of comparative literature. Conceived as an aesthetic project but born into political realities, comparative literature has struggled to achieve the impartial perspective that Schiller (and behind him, Kant) advocated. Yet this still could, and arguably should, be its aim: to outgrow its politicized history and create a fully egalitarian, disinterested model of comparison, one in which the free 'play' of literature embraces all peoples equally, regardless of national history or linguistic status. Comparative literature developed as the study of writing across borders, but it has yet to conceive a world *without* borders. If it is self-evident that such an aim can never be fully realized, such is the open-ended nature of education, conceived in its true etymological sense (*e-ducare*) as a process of 'leading people out'.

It is also the nature of capitalism. Comparative literature is nothing if not market-driven, and dewy-eyed notions of the free play of comparison quickly founder on hard-nosed commercial considerations. A whole host of sociological factors determine what internationally minded readers want—levels of education, travel experiences, the funding and marketing of literary translation—but critical theories are surely a long way down the list. The reality is that cultural differences are more perceived than understood; publishers pander, as they must, to clichés and preconceptions. For all the academic obsession with the 'Other', many readers are looking for more of the same, for confirmation of the supposedly universal feelings to be found in literature from one end of the globe to the other. Commercial realities, in this sense, are beyond compare.

It is precisely for this reason, however, that the concept of comparative literature is so necessary. Its task is to work with, but also against, commercial preconceptions; to take questions from one culture and pose them to another; and to ensure the good faith even of bad writing. This onus of evaluation sometimes gets lost in critical discussions of the discipline; but who else is to assess the best and worst of world literature if not comparatists? If international prizes are not to be decided on merely political grounds, then critically informed comparison is essential. In the ecology of books, comparative literature has a pragmatic, as well as a professorial role to play.

Such pragmatism extends, of course, to the increasingly important sphere of 'digital Humanities'. By nature interdisciplinary, digitized approaches to the Humanist tradition—whether in the form of online editions or bibliographical diagrams, computer databases or Internet encyclopaedia—tend to the maximal, pursuing ever-bigger data. In a world in which more and more information requires synthesizing, comparison remains the one indispensable tool. Indeed, the striking thing, in many ways, is just how much the 21st-century approach to information echoes that of the 19th: digital humanists are essentially philologists with computers, digging under cultures with their keyboards. The philology of the future is also the philology of the past; Ernest Renan's claim that 'comparison is the great instrument of criticism' remains as true now as it was in 1848.

The big difference between then and now, of course, is the sheer amount of information at our disposal. Already in 1935 Paul Valéry, when attempting an assessment of the modern mind, could state that 'all knowledge today is necessarily comparative knowledge'; it barely needs stating how much truer this is almost a century later. In the age of the Internet, the trick for the comparatist is not just knowing what to compare, but also what *not* to compare. If 'comp lit' is not to turn into 'comp list', with texts and authors simply piled up *ad nauseam* by a computer, then human judgement remains indispensable. With vast amounts of information instantly available, contemporary comparative literature is not so much about retrieving content as about knowing where to look in the first place; Brandes' image of the comparatist's telescope might now be better reconfigured as a kaleidoscope, refracting knowledge in every possible direction. Flooded with data, perspective is at an all-time premium.

Yet such an information overload is characteristic, ultimately, not just of our own, multimedia era, but also of modernity as a whole. It is no coincidence that the discipline of comparative literature began as modernity began, in the post-Revolutionary fervour of the early 1800s. The increasing prominence of comparison as an interpretive model accompanied the increasing proliferation of information in the 19th century; the more people knew about other cultures, the more they compared. That they still imposed their own prejudices on this knowledge tells us as much about human nature as about comparative literature, but it does not diminish the increasing importance of comparison to the modern age. How, indeed, can one even understand one's era as modern, unless it is by implicitly comparing it with the past? Modernity, like Antiquity, is a comparative concept.

It may be, in short, that comparative literature needs to understand itself more comparatively. Cognate approaches to other disciplines—comparative history, comparative law, comparative politics—are often considerably firmer in their grasp of their own methodology, triangulating themselves more rigorously within the sphere of global relations. Whether pursued as close or as distant reading, as creative practice or as critical theory, comparative literature can surely learn from the global history approach to the universalization of ideas, or from the social sciences approach to the ways in which information circulates—with the aim not of abjuring its Humanist mission, but of expanding it. If comparison is ubiquitous, literary studies must consider what it can learn from looking beyond literature.

For what remains most surprising is just how much comparative literature in the 21st century hides in plain sight. Its practice is everywhere, the very basis for how we gather knowledge; its practitioners, however, often struggle to attain the visibility of critics based within one language, torn as they necessarily are between competing traditions. Many of the most prominent comparatists are not even known under this name, but figure rather as literary theorists, cultural critics, or eccentric polymaths. It is in the interests of comparative literature that this situation change, and that its leading exponents gain prominence *as comparatists* in the public, as well as in the professorial, sphere. As the most demanding of literary disciplines, comparative literature should attract the brightest, most ambitious students; but aspiring comparatists need role models, and they are not always apparent in literary debate, dominated as it is by national traditions heavily invested in their own primacy. It is striking, if perhaps unsurprising, how many leading comparatists grew up in multilingual environments (comparative literature is in this sense among the most personal, as well as the most political, of intellectual activities). With the right role models, however, anyone can aspire to a multipolar perspective. Emerging from the profoundly monocultural world of the British education system, I for one was inspired by the likes of George Steiner or Edward Said to discover other literary traditions, and to explore the essential interconnectedness of all cultures; the initial difficulty, the challenge to raise my sights beyond my comfort zone, was part of the appeal. Such exemplars are sorely required in present times. Cosmopolitanism, especially in the Anglo-Saxon world, needs all the support it can get.

Comparing literatures is a complex process, fraught with theoretical, practical, and political dangers. Its ambition, however, is a simple one: to understand the ways in which literary cultures interact. As the discipline moves ever further away from its European origins, the future of comparative literature depends on retaining this coherence despite its worldwide reach, on articulating its place at the centre of the Humanities, and on making intellectual virtues out of institutional necessities. If comparative literature is to become the philology of the future, it must build on the achievements of the past, while working within the structures of the present. From politics to philosophy, from history to linguistics, comparatists have always drawn on the broadest possible range of approaches to culture; in this age of specialists, generalists continue to play a vital role in shaping and supporting the life of the mind. International, interdisciplinary forms of knowledge remain, in short, the very essence of modernity. Now more than ever, the aesthetic education of comparative literature is indispensable.

References and further reading

General sources and anthologies

Damrosch, David, Melas, Natalie, and Buthelezi, Mbongiseni (eds), *The Princeton Sourcebook in Comparative Literature* (Princeton, 2009)
D'haen, Theo, Damrosch, David, and Kadir, Djelal (eds), *Routledge Companion to World Literature* (Routledge, 2012)
Schulz, Hans-Joachim, and Rhein, Philip H. (eds), *Comparative Literature: The Early Years* (University of North Carolina, 1973)

Introductions to comparative literature

Bassnett, Susan, *Comparative Literature* (Blackwell, 1993)
Domínguez, César, Saussy, Haun, and Villanueva, Darío, *Introducing Comparative Literature: New Trends and Applications* (Routledge, 2015)
Morgan, Ben, Omri, Mohamed-Salah, and Reynolds, Matthew, 'Comparative Criticism: Histories and Methods', *Comparative Critical Studies* 12/2 (June 2015), 147–59

Principles and practices

Aristotle, *Poetics* (Penguin, 1996)
Bloom, Harold, *The Western Canon* (Harcourt Brace, 1994)
Borges, Jorge Luis, *Pierre Menard, Author of* Don Quixote (1939), tr. Andrew Hurley (Penguin, 1998), 88–95

Bouju, Emmanuel, 'Achille et la tortue. Quelques considérations intempestives sur la périodisation de la littérature', *Le temps des lettres. Quelles périodisations pour l'histoire de la littérature française du XXe siècle?*, ed. Fr. Dugast and M. Touret (Rennes, 2001), 45–54

Cervantes, Miguel de, *Don Quixote*, tr. John Rutherford (Penguin, 2003)

Damrosch, David, 'World Literature in a Postcanonical, Hypercanonical Age', *Comparative Literature in an Age of Globalization*, ed. Haun Saussy (Johns Hopkins University Press, 2006), 43–53

Dowden, Edward, *Shakspere: A Primer* (Macmillan, 1922)

Eliot, T.S., 'Tradition and the Individual Talent', *The Sacred Wood* (Methuen, 1945), 47–59

Ferris, David, 'Indiscipline', *Comparative Literature in an Age of Globalization* (Johns Hopkins University Press, 1994), 78–99

Lewis, Martin W., and Wigen, Kären, *The Myth of Continents: A Critique of Metageography* (University of California Press, 1997)

Lukács, Georg, *Studies in European Realism* (Merlin, 1972)

Moretti, Franco, *Signs taken for Wonders: On the Sociology of Literary Forms* (Verso, 2005)

Moretti, Franco, *Graphs, Maps, Trees: Abstract Models for Literary History* (Verso, 2005)

Moretti, Franco, *Distant Reading: The Formation of an Unorthodox Literary Critic* (Verso, 2013)

Pollock, Sheldon, 'Cosmopolitanism, Vernacularism, and Pre-modernity', *Global Intellectual History*, ed. Samuel Moyn and Andrew Sartori (Columbia, 2013), 59–80

Schaffner, Anna Katharina, and Weller, Shane (eds), *Modernist Eroticisms: European Literature after Sexology* (Palgrave Macmillan, 2012)

Steiner, George, *The Death of Tragedy* (Yale, 1996)

Stuurman, Siep, 'Common Humanity and Cultural Difference on the Sedentary-Nomadic Frontier: Herodotus, Sima Qian, and Ibn Khaldun', *Global Intellectual History*, ed. Samuel Moyn and Andrew Sartori (Columbia, 2013), 33–58

Szondi, Peter, *An Essay on the Tragic*, tr. Paul Fleming (Stanford, 2002)

Thiong'o, Ngũgĩ wa, *Decolonising the Mind: The Politics of Language in African Literature* (Heinemann Educational, 1986)

Underwood, Ted, *Why Literary Periods Mattered: Historical Contrast and the Prestige of English Studies* (Stanford, 2013)

Gilgamesh

Cregan-Reid, Vybarr, *Discovering Gilgamesh* (Manchester University Press, 2013)
Damrosch, David, *The Buried Book: The Loss and Rediscovery of the Great Epic of Gilgamesh* (Henry Holt, 2007)
Smith, George, 'The Chaldean Account of the Deluge', in *Transactions of the Society of Biblical Archaeology* 1–2 (1872), 213–34

Philology and German comparative literature

Benes, Tuska, *In Babel's Shadow: Language, Philology, and the Nation in Nineteenth-Century Germany* (Wayne State University Press, 2008)
Herder, Johann Gottfried, *Philosophical Writings*, tr. Michael N. Forster (CUP, 2002)
Lepper, Marcel, *Philologie. Eine Einführung* (Junius, 2014)
Turner, James, *Philology: The Forgotten Origins of the Modern Humanities* (Princeton, 2014), esp. ch. 5

Russian and Eastern European comparative literature

Dobrenko, Evgeny and Tihanov, Galin, *A History of Russian Literary Theory and Criticism: The Soviet Age and Beyond* (University of Pittsburgh Press, 2011)
Emerson, Caryl, 'Answering for Central and Eastern Europe', *Comparative Literature in an Age of Globalization*, ed. Haun Saussy (Johns Hopkins University Press, 2006), 203–11
Gould, Rebecca, *Writers and Rebels: The Literature of Insurgency in the Caucasus* (Yale, 2016)
Polonsky, Rachel, *English Literature and the Russian Aesthetic Renaissance* (CUP, 1998)
Szerb, Antal, *Reflections in the Library: Selected Literary Essays 1926–1944*, tr. Peter Sherwood (Legenda, 2017)

Danish comparative literature

Larsen, Svend Erik, 'Georg Brandes: The Telescope of Comparative Literature', *The Routledge Companion to World Literature* (Routledge, 2012)

Thomsen, Mads Rosendahl, and Ringgaard, Dan (eds), *Danish Literature as World Literature* (Bloomsbury, 2017)
Weinstein, Arnold, *Northern Arts: The Breakthrough of Scandinavian Literature and Art, from Ibsen to Bergman* (Princeton, 2008)

French comparative literature

Brunetière, Ferdinand, *L'Évolution des genres dans l'histoire de la littérature* (Hachette, 1914)
Chasles, Philarète, 'Foreign Literature Compared', in Hans-Joachim Schulz and Philip H. Rhein (eds), *Comparative Literature: The Early Years* (University of North Carolina, 1973), 16–37
Etiemble, René, *Comparaison n'est pas raison. La crise de la littérature comparée* (Gallimard, 1963)
Noël, François-Joseph-Michel, and de La Place, Guislain-François-Marie-Joseph (eds), *Leçons françaises de littérature et de morale* (Le Normant, 1816)
Renan, Ernest, *The Future of Science: Ideas of 1848*, tr. Albert Vandam and C.B. Pitman (Chapman & Hall, 1891)
Tageldin, Shaden M., 'One Comparative Literature? "Birth" of a Discipline in French-Egyptian Translation, 1810–1834', *Comparative Literature Studies* 47/4 (2000), 417–45

Hispanic comparative literature

Andrade, Oswald de, 'Cannibalist Manifesto', tr. Leslie Bary, *Latin American Literary Review* 19/38 (1991), 38–47
Castro, Américo, *The Spaniards: An Introduction to their History*, tr. Willard F. King (University of California Press, 1971)
Guillén, Claudio, *The Challenge of Comparative Literature*, tr. Cola Franzen (Harvard, 1993)
Novillo-Corvalán, Patricia, *Modernism and Latin America: Transnational Networks of Literary Exchange* (Routledge, 2018)

American comparative literature

Bernheimer, Charles (ed.), *Comparative Literature in the Age of Multiculturalism* (Johns Hopkins University Press, 1994)
de Man, Paul, *The Paul de Man Notebooks*, ed. Martin McQuillan (Edinburgh University Press, 2014), esp. 'Part III: Teaching'

Emerson, Ralph Waldo, *Representative Men* (Belknap Press, 1996)
Gayley, Charles Mills, 'What is Comparative Literature' (1903), *The Princeton Sourcebook in Comparative Literature* (Princeton, 2009), 67–78
Saussy, Haun (ed.), *Comparative Literature in an Age of Globalization* (Johns Hopkins University Press, 2006)
Wellek, René, 'The Crisis of Comparative Literature', *The Princeton Sourcebook in Comparative Literature* (Princeton, 2009), 161–72
Wellek, René, 'The Name and Nature of Comparative Literature', *Discriminations: Further Concepts of Criticism* (University of North Carolina Press, 1970), 1–36
Wellek, René, 'The New Nihilism in Literary Studies', in *Aesthetics and the Literature of Ideas: Essays in Honour of A. Owen Aldridge* (University of Delaware, 1990)

'European' literature

Auerbach, Ernst, *Mimesis: The Representation of Reality in Western Literature*, tr. Willard R. Trask (Princeton, 2003)
Auerbach, Ernst, 'The Philology of World Literature', *Time, History, and Literature: Selected Essays of Erich Auerbach* (Princeton, 2013), 253–65
Babits, Mihály, *Geschichte der europäischen Literatur* (Europa, 1949)
Cohen, Walter, *A History of European Literature* (OUP, 2017)
Coleridge, S.T., *Aids to Reflection*, vol. 1 (Pickering, 1848), 176–7
Coudenhove-Kalergi, Richard von, *Pan-Europe* (Knopf, 1926)
Curtius, Ernst Robert, *European Literature and the Latin Middle Ages*, tr. Willard R. Trask (Princeton, 1952)
de Man, Paul, *Allegories of Reading: Figural Language in Rousseau, Nietzsche, Rilke, and Proust* (Yale, 1979)
Hutchinson, Ben, *Lateness and Modern European Literature* (OUP, 2016)
Hutchinson, Ben, 'Late Reading: Erich Auerbach and the *Spätboot* of Comparative Literature', *Comparative Critical Studies* 14/1 (2017), 69–85
Macaulay Posnett, Hutcheson, *Comparative Literature* (Kegan Paul, Trench & Co, 1886)
Spengler, Oswald, *The Decline of the West*, tr. Charles Atkinson (OUP, 1991)

Spitzer, Leo, *Linguistics and Literary History* (Princeton, 1967)
Steiner, George, *Errata: An Examined Life* (Yale, 1999)
Valéry, Paul, 'The Crisis of the Mind', *Paul Valéry: An Anthology* (Princeton, 1977)

World literature

Apter, Emily, *Against World Literature: On the Politics of Untranslatability* (Verso, 2013)
Casanova, Pascale, *The World Republic of Letters* (Harvard, 2007)
Cheah, Pheng, *What is a World? On Postcolonial Literature as World Literature* (Duke, 2016)
Damrosch, David, *What is World Literature?* (Princeton, 2003)
Damrosch, David, *World Literature in Theory* (Wiley-Blackwell, 2014)
Goethe, Johann Wolfgang von, *Conversations of Goethe with Eckermann and Soret*, tr. John Oxenford (CUP, 2012)
Barbery, Muriel, Ben Jelloun, Tahar, Borer, Alain, et al., 'Pour une littérature-monde en Français', *Le Monde* 15 March 2007 (see: <http://www.lemonde.fr/livres/article/2007/03/15/des-ecrivains-plaident-pour-un-roman-en-francais-ouvert-sur-le-monde_883572_3260.html)>
Spivak, Gayatri Chakravorty, *Death of a Discipline* (Columbia, 2003)
Szerb, Antal, *Geschichte der Weltliteratur* (Schwabe, 2016)
Tagore, Rabindranath, 'World Literature', in *Rabindranath Tagore: Selected Writings on Literature and Language*, ed. Sukanta Chaudhuri (OUP, 2001), 147–9
Thomsen, Mads Rosendahl, *Mapping World Literature: International Canonization and Transnational Literatures* (Bloomsbury, 2008)
Thornber, Karen Laura, *Empire of Texts in Motion: Chinese, Korean, and Taiwanese Transculturations of Japanese Literature* (Harvard, 2009)

Literary theory

Barthes, Roland, *Writing Degree Zero*, tr. Annette Lavers and Colin Smith (Hill & Wang, 1977)
Cixous, Hélène, 'The Laugh of the Medusa', tr. Keith Cohen and Paula Cohen, *Signs* 1/4 (Summer 1976), 875–93
Derrida, Jacques, 'Différance', *Margins of Philosophy*, tr. Alan Bass (University of Chicago, 1982), 3–27

Derrida, Jacques, *Of Grammatology*, tr. G.C. Spivak (Johns Hopkins University Press, 1998)
Eagleton, Terry, *Literary Theory: An Introduction* (Blackwell, 1983)
Gilbert, Sandra, and Gubar, Susan, *The Madwoman in the Attic: The Woman Writer and the Nineteenth-Century Literary Imagination* (Yale, 1979)

Cultural studies

Barthes, Roland, *Mythologies*, tr. Annette Lavers (Farrar, Strauss & Giroux, 1972)
During, Simon (ed.), *The Cultural Studies Reader* (Routledge, 1993)
Eliot, T.S., *Notes Towards the Definition of Culture* (Faber & Faber, 1973)
Hall, Stuart, *Cultural Studies 1983: A Theoretical History* (Duke University Press, 2016)
Hall, Stuart, *Familiar Stranger: A Life between Two Islands* (Allen Lane, 2017)
Hoggart, Richard, *The Uses of Literacy: Aspects of Working-Class Life* (Penguin, 2009)

Postcolonialism

Aravamudan, Srinivas, *Enlightenment Orientalism* (Chicago, 2011)
Bhabha, Homi, *The Location of Culture* (Routledge, 2004)
Césaire, Aimé, *Discourse on Colonialism*, tr. Joan Pinkham (Monthly Review Press, 2000)
Césaire, Aimé, *Return to my Native Land*, tr. Mireille Rosello and Annie Pritchard (Bloodaxe, 1995)
Chakrabarty, Dipesh, *Provincializing Europe: Postcolonial Thought and Historical Difference* (Princeton, 2000)
Fanon, Frantz, *The Wretched of the Earth*, tr. Richard Philcox (Grove, 2005)
Glissant, Édouard, 'Cross-Cultural Poetics: National Literatures', *The Princeton Sourcebook in Comparative Literature* (Princeton, 2009), 248–58
Li, Xiofan Amy (ed.), 'The Exotic and the Autoexotic', *Publications of the Modern Language Association of America* 132/2 (March 2017), 392–461
Said, Edward, *Orientalism* (Pantheon, 1978)

Translation theory

Apter, Emily, *The Translation Zone: A New Comparative Literature* (Princeton, 2005)

Benjamin, Walter, 'The Task of the Translator', *Illuminations*, tr. Harry Zohn (Fontana, 1992), 70–82

Cassin, Barbara (ed.), *Dictionary of Untranslatables: A Philosophical Lexicon* (Princeton, 2014)

Evan-Zohar, Itamar, 'The Position of Translated Literature within the Literary Polysystem', *Papers in Historical Poetics* (Porter Institute, 1978)

Liu, Lydia H., *Translingual Practice: Literature, National Culture, and Translated Modernity—China, 1900–1937* (Stanford, 1995)

Reynolds, Matthew, *Translation: A Very Short Introduction* (OUP, 2016)

Steiner, George, *After Babel* (OUP, 1975)

Taylor, Charles, *The Language Animal: The Full Shape of the Human Linguistic Capacity* (Harvard, 2016)

Reception studies

Bloom, Harold, *The Anxiety of Influence: A Theory of Poetry* (OUP, 1973)

Fumaroli, Marc (ed.), *La Querelle des anciens et des modernes* (Gallimard Folio, 2001)

Hardwick, Lorna, and Stray, Christopher (eds), *A Companion to Classical Receptions* (Wiley-Blackwell, 2007)

Horace, *Satires and Epistles*, tr. John Davie (Oxford World's Classics, 2011)

Skinner, Quentin, 'Meaning and Understanding in the History of Ideas', *History and Theory* 8/1 (1969), 3–53

Warner, Marina, *Stranger Magic: Charmed States and the Arabian Nights* (Chatto & Windus, 2011)

Zajko, Vanda (ed.), *A Handbook to the Reception of Classical Mythology* (Wiley-Blackwell, 2017)

Futures of comparative literature

Berman, Jessica, *Modernist Commitments: Ethics, Politics, and Transnational Modernism* (Columbia, 2011)

Forster, E.M., *Howard's End* (Penguin, 1961)

Pollock, Sheldon, ‘Future Philology? The Fate of a Soft Science in a Hard World’, *Critical Inquiry* 35/4 (Summer 2009), 931–61

Saussy, Haun, ‘Exquisite Cadavers Stitched from Fresh Nightmares’, *Comparative Literature in an Age of Globalization* (Johns Hopkins, 2006), 3–42

Saussy, Haun, ‘Comparative Literature: The Next Ten Years’: <https://stateofthediscipline.acla.org/entry/comparative-literature-next-ten-years>

Schiller, Friedrich, *On the Aesthetic Education of Man*, ed. E.M. Wilkinson and L.A. Willoughby (OUP, 1983)

Seigel, Micol, ‘Beyond Compare: Comparative Method after the Transnational Turn’, *Radical History Review* 91 (Winter 2005), 62–90

Stanford Friedman, Susan, *Planetary Modernisms: Provocations on Modernity Across Time* (Columbia, 2015)

Szegedy-Maszák, Mihály, ‘Unseen Paintings and Unheard Melodies: The Uses and Limits of Interart Studies’, *Comparative Critical Studies* 12/2 (2015), 251–66

Valéry, Paul, ‘Le bilan de l’intelligence’, *Œuvres*, vol. 1 (Gallimard, 1957)

Websites

American Comparative Literature Association: <www.acla.org>

British Comparative Literature Association: <www.bcla.org>

Index

A

B

F

G

H

O

P

Q

R

S

T

U

V

W

CONFUCIANISM Daniel K. Gardner
THE CONQUISTADORS
Matthew Restall and
Felipe Fernández-Armesto
CONSCIENCE Paul Strohm
CONSCIOUSNESS Susan Blackmore
CONTEMPORARY ART
Julian Stallabrass
CONTEMPORARY FICTION
Robert Eaglestone
CONTINENTAL PHILOSOPHY
Simon Critchley
COPERNICUS Owen Gingerich
CORAL REEFS Charles Sheppard
CORPORATE SOCIAL
RESPONSIBILITY Jeremy Moon
CORRUPTION Leslie Holmes
COSMOLOGY Peter Coles
CRIME FICTION Richard Bradford
CRIMINAL JUSTICE Julian V. Roberts
CRITICAL THEORY
Stephen Eric Bronner
THE CRUSADES Christopher Tyerman
CRYPTOGRAPHY Fred Piper and
Sean Murphy
CRYSTALLOGRAPHY A. M. Glazer
THE CULTURAL REVOLUTION
Richard Curt Kraus
DADA AND SURREALISM
David Hopkins
DANTE Peter Hainsworth and
David Robey
DARWIN Jonathan Howard
THE DEAD SEA SCROLLS
Timothy H. Lim
DECOLONIZATION Dane Kennedy
DEMOCRACY Bernard Crick
DEPRESSION Jan Scott and
Mary Jane Tacchi
DERRIDA Simon Glendinning
DESCARTES Tom Sorell
DESERTS Nick Middleton
DESIGN John Heskett
DEVELOPMENTAL BIOLOGY
Lewis Wolpert
THE DEVIL Darren Oldridge
DIASPORA Kevin Kenny
DICTIONARIES Lynda Mugglestone
DINOSAURS David Norman
DIPLOMACY Joseph M. Siracusa
DOCUMENTARY FILM
Patricia Aufderheide
DREAMING J. Allan Hobson
DRUGS Les Iversen
DRUIDS Barry Cunliffe
EARLY MUSIC Thomas Forrest Kelly
THE EARTH Martin Redfern
EARTH SYSTEM SCIENCE Tim Lenton
ECONOMICS Partha Dasgupta
EDUCATION Gary Thomas
EGYPTIAN MYTH Geraldine Pinch
EIGHTEENTH-CENTURY
BRITAIN Paul Langford
THE ELEMENTS Philip Ball
EMOTION Dylan Evans
EMPIRE Stephen Howe
ENGELS Terrell Carver
ENGINEERING David Blockley
THE ENGLISH LANGUAGE
Simon Horobin
ENGLISH LITERATURE Jonathan Bate
THE ENLIGHTENMENT
John Robertson
ENTREPRENEURSHIP Paul Westhead
and Mike Wright
ENVIRONMENTAL
ECONOMICS Stephen Smith
ENVIRONMENTAL LAW
Elizabeth Fisher
ENVIRONMENTAL
POLITICS Andrew Dobson
EPICUREANISM Catherine Wilson
EPIDEMIOLOGY Rodolfo Saracci
ETHICS Simon Blackburn
ETHNOMUSICOLOGY Timothy Rice
THE ETRUSCANS Christopher Smith
EUGENICS Philippa Levine
THE EUROPEAN UNION John Pinder
and Simon Usherwood
EUROPEAN UNION LAW
Anthony Arnull
EVOLUTION Brian and
Deborah Charlesworth
EXISTENTIALISM Thomas Flynn
EXPLORATION Stewart A. Weaver
THE EYE Michael Land
FAIRY TALE Marina Warner
FAMILY LAW Jonathan Herring
FASCISM Kevin Passmore
FASHION Rebecca Arnold

ARISTOCRACY William Doyle
ARISTOTLE Jonathan Barnes
ART HISTORY Dana Arnold
ART THEORY Cynthia Freeland
ASIAN AMERICAN HISTORY Madeline Y. Hsu
ASTROBIOLOGY David C. Catling
ASTROPHYSICS James Binney
ATHEISM Julian Baggini
THE ATMOSPHERE Paul I. Palmer
AUGUSTINE Henry Chadwick
AUSTRALIA Kenneth Morgan
AUTISM Uta Frith
THE AVANT GARDE David Cottington
THE AZTECS Davíd Carrasco
BABYLONIA Trevor Bryce
BACTERIA Sebastian G. B. Amyes
BANKING John Goddard and John O. S. Wilson
BARTHES Jonathan Culler
THE BEATS David Sterritt
BEAUTY Roger Scruton
BEHAVIOURAL ECONOMICS Michelle Baddeley
BESTSELLERS John Sutherland
THE BIBLE John Riches
BIBLICAL ARCHAEOLOGY Eric H. Cline
BIG DATA Dawn E. Holmes
BIOGRAPHY Hermione Lee
BLACK HOLES Katherine Blundell
BLOOD Chris Cooper
THE BLUES Elijah Wald
THE BODY Chris Shilling
THE BOOK OF MORMON Terryl Givens
BORDERS Alexander C. Diener and Joshua Hagen
THE BRAIN Michael O'Shea
BRANDING Robert Jones
THE BRICS Andrew F. Cooper
THE BRITISH CONSTITUTION Martin Loughlin
THE BRITISH EMPIRE Ashley Jackson
BRITISH POLITICS Anthony Wright
BUDDHA Michael Carrithers
BUDDHISM Damien Keown
BUDDHIST ETHICS Damien Keown
BYZANTIUM Peter Sarris
CALVINISM Jon Balserak
CANCER Nicholas James
CAPITALISM James Fulcher
CATHOLICISM Gerald O'Collins
CAUSATION Stephen Mumford and Rani Lill Anjum
THE CELL Terence Allen and Graham Cowling
THE CELTS Barry Cunliffe
CHAOS Leonard Smith
CHEMISTRY Peter Atkins
CHILD PSYCHOLOGY Usha Goswami
CHILDREN'S LITERATURE Kimberley Reynolds
CHINESE LITERATURE Sabina Knight
CHOICE THEORY Michael Allingham
CHRISTIAN ART Beth Williamson
CHRISTIAN ETHICS D. Stephen Long
CHRISTIANITY Linda Woodhead
CIRCADIAN RHYTHMS Russell Foster and Leon Kreitzman
CITIZENSHIP Richard Bellamy
CIVIL ENGINEERING David Muir Wood
CLASSICAL LITERATURE William Allan
CLASSICAL MYTHOLOGY Helen Morales
CLASSICS Mary Beard and John Henderson
CLAUSEWITZ Michael Howard
CLIMATE Mark Maslin
CLIMATE CHANGE Mark Maslin
CLINICAL PSYCHOLOGY Susan Llewelyn and Katie Aafjes-van Doorn
COGNITIVE NEUROSCIENCE Richard Passingham
THE COLD WAR Robert McMahon
COLONIAL AMERICA Alan Taylor
COLONIAL LATIN AMERICAN LITERATURE Rolena Adorno
COMBINATORICS Robin Wilson
COMEDY Matthew Bevis
COMMUNISM Leslie Holmes
COMPARATIVE LITERATURE Ben Hutchinson
COMPLEXITY John H. Holland
THE COMPUTER Darrel Ince
COMPUTER SCIENCE Subrata Dasgupta

Y

Z

BESTSELLERS

A Very Short Introduction

John Sutherland

'I rejoice', said Doctor Johnson, 'to concur with the Common Reader.' For the last century, the tastes and preferences of the common reader have been reflected in the American and British bestseller lists, and this *Very Short Introduction* takes an engaging look through the lists to reveal what we have been reading - and why. John Sutherland shows that bestseller lists monitor one of the strongest pulses in modern literature and are therefore worthy of serious study. Along the way, he lifts the lid on the bestseller industry, examines what makes a book into a bestseller, and asks what separates bestsellers from canonical fiction.

> 'His amiable trawl through the history of popular books is frequently entertaining'
>
> Scott Pack, The Times

www.oup.com/vsi

ENGLISH LITERATURE

A Very Short Introduction

Jonathan Bate

Sweeping across two millennia and every literary genre, acclaimed scholar and biographer Jonathan Bate provides a dazzling introduction to English Literature. The focus is wide, shifting from the birth of the novel and the brilliance of English comedy to the deep Englishness of landscape poetry and the ethnic diversity of Britain's Nobel literature laureates. It goes on to provide a more in-depth analysis, with close readings from an extraordinary scene in King Lear to a war poem by Carol Ann Duffy, and a series of striking examples of how literary texts change as they are transmitted from writer to reader.

{No reviews}

www.oup.com/vsi

French Literature

A Very Short Introduction

John D. Lyons

The heritage of literature in the French language is rich, varied, and extensive in time and space; appealing both to its immediate public, readers of French, and also to aglobal audience reached through translations and film adaptations. *French Literature: A Very Short Introduction* introduces this lively literary world by focusing on texts - epics, novels, plays, poems, and screenplays - that concern protagonists whose adventures and conflicts reveal shifts in literary and social practices. From the hero of the medieval *Song of Roland* to the Caribbean heroines of *Tituba, Black Witch of Salem* or the European expatriate in Japan in *Fear and Trembling*, these problematic protagonists allow us to understand what interests writers and readers across the wide world of French.

www.oup.com/vsi

ANALYTIC PHILOSOPHY Michael Beaney
ANARCHISM Alex Prichard
ANCIENT ASSYRIA Karen Radner
ANCIENT EGYPT Ian Shaw
ANCIENT EGYPTIAN ART AND ARCHITECTURE Christina Riggs
ANCIENT GREECE Paul Cartledge
ANCIENT GREEK AND ROMAN SCIENCE Liba Taub
THE ANCIENT NEAR EAST Amanda H. Podany
ANCIENT PHILOSOPHY Julia Annas
ANCIENT WARFARE Harry Sidebottom
ANGELS David Albert Jones
ANGLICANISM Mark Chapman
THE ANGLO-SAXON AGE John Blair
ANIMAL BEHAVIOUR Tristram D. Wyatt
THE ANIMAL KINGDOM Peter Holland
ANIMAL RIGHTS David DeGrazia
ANSELM Thomas Williams
THE ANTARCTIC Klaus Dodds
ANTHROPOCENE Erle C. Ellis
ANTISEMITISM Steven Beller
ANXIETY Daniel Freeman and Jason Freeman
THE APOCRYPHAL GOSPELS Paul Foster
APPLIED MATHEMATICS Alain Goriely
THOMAS AQUINAS Fergus Kerr
ARBITRATION Thomas Schultz and Thomas Grant
ARCHAEOLOGY Paul Bahn
ARCHITECTURE Andrew Ballantyne
THE ARCTIC Klaus Dodds and Jamie Woodward
HANNAH ARENDT Dana Villa
ARISTOCRACY William Doyle
ARISTOTLE Jonathan Barnes
ART HISTORY Dana Arnold
ART THEORY Cynthia Freeland
ARTIFICIAL INTELLIGENCE Margaret A. Boden
ASIAN AMERICAN HISTORY Madeline Y. Hsu
ASTROBIOLOGY David C. Catling
ASTROPHYSICS James Binney
ATHEISM Julian Baggini
THE ATMOSPHERE Paul I. Palmer
AUGUSTINE Henry Chadwick
JANE AUSTEN Tom Keymer
AUSTRALIA Kenneth Morgan
AUTISM Uta Frith
AUTOBIOGRAPHY Laura Marcus
THE AVANT GARDE David Cottington
THE AZTECS Davíd Carrasco
BABYLONIA Trevor Bryce
BACTERIA Sebastian G. B. Amyes
BANKING John Goddard and John O. S. Wilson
BARTHES Jonathan Culler
THE BEATS David Sterritt
BEAUTY Roger Scruton
LUDWIG VAN BEETHOVEN Mark Evan Bonds
BEHAVIOURAL ECONOMICS Michelle Baddeley
BESTSELLERS John Sutherland
THE BIBLE John Riches
BIBLICAL ARCHAEOLOGY Eric H. Cline
BIG DATA Dawn E. Holmes
BIOCHEMISTRY Mark Lorch
BIODIVERSITY CONSERVATION David Macdonald
BIOGEOGRAPHY Mark V. Lomolino
BIOGRAPHY Hermione Lee
BIOMETRICS Michael Fairhurst
ELIZABETH BISHOP Jonathan F. S. Post
BLACK HOLES Katherine Blundell
BLASPHEMY Yvonne Sherwood
BLOOD Chris Cooper
THE BLUES Elijah Wald
THE BODY Chris Shilling
THE BOHEMIANS David Weir
NIELS BOHR J. L. Heilbron
THE BOOK OF COMMON PRAYER Brian Cummings
THE BOOK OF MORMON Terryl Givens
BORDERS Alexander C. Diener and Joshua Hagen
THE BRAIN Michael O'Shea
BRANDING Robert Jones
THE BRICS Andrew F. Cooper

BRITISH CINEMA Charles Barr
THE BRITISH CONSTITUTION Martin Loughlin
THE BRITISH EMPIRE Ashley Jackson
BRITISH POLITICS Tony Wright
BUDDHA Michael Carrithers
BUDDHISM Damien Keown
BUDDHIST ETHICS Damien Keown
BYZANTIUM Peter Sarris
CALVINISM Jon Balserak
ALBERT CAMUS Oliver Gloag
CANADA Donald Wright
CANCER Nicholas James
CAPITALISM James Fulcher
CATHOLICISM Gerald O'Collins
CAUSATION Stephen Mumford and Rani Lill Anjum
THE CELL Terence Allen and Graham Cowling
THE CELTS Barry Cunliffe
CHAOS Leonard Smith
GEOFFREY CHAUCER David Wallace
CHEMISTRY Peter Atkins
CHILD PSYCHOLOGY Usha Goswami
CHILDREN'S LITERATURE Kimberley Reynolds
CHINESE LITERATURE Sabina Knight
CHOICE THEORY Michael Allingham
CHRISTIAN ART Beth Williamson
CHRISTIAN ETHICS D. Stephen Long
CHRISTIANITY Linda Woodhead
CIRCADIAN RHYTHMS Russell Foster and Leon Kreitzman
CITIZENSHIP Richard Bellamy
CITY PLANNING Carl Abbott
CIVIL ENGINEERING David Muir Wood
THE CIVIL RIGHTS MOVEMENT Thomas C. Holt
CLASSICAL LITERATURE William Allan
CLASSICAL MYTHOLOGY Helen Morales
CLASSICS Mary Beard and John Henderson
CLAUSEWITZ Michael Howard
CLIMATE Mark Maslin
CLIMATE CHANGE Mark Maslin
CLINICAL PSYCHOLOGY Susan Llewelyn and Katie Aafjes-van Doorn
COGNITIVE BEHAVIOURAL THERAPY Freda McManus
COGNITIVE NEUROSCIENCE Richard Passingham
THE COLD WAR Robert J. McMahon
COLONIAL AMERICA Alan Taylor
COLONIAL LATIN AMERICAN LITERATURE Rolena Adorno
COMBINATORICS Robin Wilson
COMEDY Matthew Bevis
COMMUNISM Leslie Holmes
COMPARATIVE LITERATURE Ben Hutchinson
COMPETITION AND ANTITRUST LAW Ariel Ezrachi
COMPLEXITY John H. Holland
THE COMPUTER Darrel Ince
COMPUTER SCIENCE Subrata Dasgupta
CONCENTRATION CAMPS Dan Stone
CONDENSED MATTER PHYSICS Ross H. McKenzie
CONFUCIANISM Daniel K. Gardner
THE CONQUISTADORS Matthew Restall and Felipe Fernández-Armesto
CONSCIENCE Paul Strohm
CONSCIOUSNESS Susan Blackmore
CONTEMPORARY ART Julian Stallabrass
CONTEMPORARY FICTION Robert Eaglestone
CONTINENTAL PHILOSOPHY Simon Critchley
COPERNICUS Owen Gingerich
CORAL REEFS Charles Sheppard
CORPORATE SOCIAL RESPONSIBILITY Jeremy Moon
CORRUPTION Leslie Holmes
COSMOLOGY Peter Coles
COUNTRY MUSIC Richard Carlin
CREATIVITY Vlad Glăveanu
CRIME FICTION Richard Bradford
CRIMINAL JUSTICE Julian V. Roberts
CRIMINOLOGY Tim Newburn
CRITICAL THEORY Stephen Eric Bronner
THE CRUSADES Christopher Tyerman

CRYPTOGRAPHY Fred Piper and Sean Murphy
CRYSTALLOGRAPHY A. M. Glazer
THE CULTURAL REVOLUTION Richard Curt Kraus
DADA AND SURREALISM David Hopkins
DANTE Peter Hainsworth and David Robey
DARWIN Jonathan Howard
THE DEAD SEA SCROLLS Timothy H. Lim
DECADENCE David Weir
DECOLONIZATION Dane Kennedy
DEMENTIA Kathleen Taylor
DEMOCRACY Naomi Zack
DEMOGRAPHY Sarah Harper
DEPRESSION Jan Scott and Mary Jane Tacchi
DERRIDA Simon Glendinning
DESCARTES Tom Sorell
DESERTS Nick Middleton
DESIGN John Heskett
DEVELOPMENT Ian Goldin
DEVELOPMENTAL BIOLOGY Lewis Wolpert
THE DEVIL Darren Oldridge
DIASPORA Kevin Kenny
CHARLES DICKENS Jenny Hartley
DICTIONARIES Lynda Mugglestone
DINOSAURS David Norman
DIPLOMATIC HISTORY Joseph M. Siracusa
DOCUMENTARY FILM Patricia Aufderheide
DREAMING J. Allan Hobson
DRUGS Les Iversen
DRUIDS Barry Cunliffe
DYNASTY Jeroen Duindam
DYSLEXIA Margaret J. Snowling
EARLY MUSIC Thomas Forrest Kelly
THE EARTH Martin Redfern
EARTH SYSTEM SCIENCE Tim Lenton
ECOLOGY Jaboury Ghazoul
ECONOMICS Partha Dasgupta
EDUCATION Gary Thomas
EGYPTIAN MYTH Geraldine Pinch
EIGHTEENTH-CENTURY BRITAIN Paul Langford
THE ELEMENTS Philip Ball
EMOTION Dylan Evans
EMPIRE Stephen Howe
EMPLOYMENT LAW David Cabrelli
ENERGY SYSTEMS Nick Jenkins
ENGELS Terrell Carver
ENGINEERING David Blockley
THE ENGLISH LANGUAGE Simon Horobin
ENGLISH LITERATURE Jonathan Bate
THE ENLIGHTENMENT John Robertson
ENTREPRENEURSHIP Paul Westhead and Mike Wright
ENVIRONMENTAL ECONOMICS Stephen Smith
ENVIRONMENTAL ETHICS Robin Attfield
ENVIRONMENTAL LAW Elizabeth Fisher
ENVIRONMENTAL POLITICS Andrew Dobson
ENZYMES Paul Engel
EPICUREANISM Catherine Wilson
EPIDEMIOLOGY Rodolfo Saracci
ETHICS Simon Blackburn
ETHNOMUSICOLOGY Timothy Rice
THE ETRUSCANS Christopher Smith
EUGENICS Philippa Levine
THE EUROPEAN UNION Simon Usherwood and John Pinder
EUROPEAN UNION LAW Anthony Arnull
EVANGELICALISM John G. Stackhouse Jr.
EVIL Luke Russell
EVOLUTION Brian and Deborah Charlesworth
EXISTENTIALISM Thomas Flynn
EXPLORATION Stewart A. Weaver
EXTINCTION Paul B. Wignall
THE EYE Michael Land
FAIRY TALE Marina Warner
FAMILY LAW Jonathan Herring
MICHAEL FARADAY Frank A. J. L. James
FASCISM Kevin Passmore
FASHION Rebecca Arnold
FEDERALISM Mark J. Rozell and Clyde Wilcox
FEMINISM Margaret Walters

FILM Michael Wood
FILM MUSIC Kathryn Kalinak
FILM NOIR James Naremore
FIRE Andrew C. Scott
THE FIRST WORLD WAR
Michael Howard
FLUID MECHANICS Eric Lauga
FOLK MUSIC Mark Slobin
FOOD John Krebs
FORENSIC PSYCHOLOGY
David Canter
FORENSIC SCIENCE Jim Fraser
FORESTS Jaboury Ghazoul
FOSSILS Keith Thomson
FOUCAULT Gary Gutting
THE FOUNDING FATHERS
R. B. Bernstein
FRACTALS Kenneth Falconer
FREE SPEECH Nigel Warburton
FREE WILL Thomas Pink
FREEMASONRY Andreas Önnerfors
FRENCH LITERATURE John D. Lyons
FRENCH PHILOSOPHY
Stephen Gaukroger and Knox Peden
THE FRENCH REVOLUTION
William Doyle
FREUD Anthony Storr
FUNDAMENTALISM Malise Ruthven
FUNGI Nicholas P. Money
THE FUTURE Jennifer M. Gidley
GALAXIES John Gribbin
GALILEO Stillman Drake
GAME THEORY Ken Binmore
GANDHI Bhikhu Parekh
GARDEN HISTORY Gordon Campbell
GENES Jonathan Slack
GENIUS Andrew Robinson
GENOMICS John Archibald
GEOGRAPHY John Matthews and
David Herbert
GEOLOGY Jan Zalasiewicz
GEOMETRY Maciej Dunajski
GEOPHYSICS William Lowrie
GEOPOLITICS Klaus Dodds
GERMAN LITERATURE Nicholas Boyle
GERMAN PHILOSOPHY
Andrew Bowie
THE GHETTO Bryan Cheyette
GLACIATION David J. A. Evans
GLOBAL CATASTROPHES Bill McGuire
GLOBAL ECONOMIC HISTORY
Robert C. Allen
GLOBAL ISLAM Nile Green
GLOBALIZATION Manfred B. Steger
GOD John Bowker
GÖDEL'S THEOREM A. W. Moore
GOETHE Ritchie Robertson
THE GOTHIC Nick Groom
GOVERNANCE Mark Bevir
GRAVITY Timothy Clifton
THE GREAT DEPRESSION AND
THE NEW DEAL Eric Rauchway
HABEAS CORPUS Amanda L. Tyler
HABERMAS James Gordon Finlayson
THE HABSBURG EMPIRE
Martyn Rady
HAPPINESS Daniel M. Haybron
THE HARLEM RENAISSANCE
Cheryl A. Wall
THE HEBREW BIBLE AS LITERATURE
Tod Linafelt
HEGEL Peter Singer
HEIDEGGER Michael Inwood
THE HELLENISTIC AGE
Peter Thonemann
HEREDITY John Waller
HERMENEUTICS
Jens Zimmermann
HERODOTUS Jennifer T. Roberts
HIEROGLYPHS Penelope Wilson
HINDUISM Kim Knott
HISTORY John H. Arnold
THE HISTORY OF ASTRONOMY
Michael Hoskin
THE HISTORY OF CHEMISTRY
William H. Brock
THE HISTORY OF CHILDHOOD
James Marten
THE HISTORY OF CINEMA
Geoffrey Nowell-Smith
THE HISTORY OF COMPUTING
Doron Swade
THE HISTORY OF EMOTIONS
Thomas Dixon
THE HISTORY OF LIFE
Michael Benton
THE HISTORY OF MATHEMATICS
Jacqueline Stedall
THE HISTORY OF MEDICINE
William Bynum

THE HISTORY OF PHYSICS J. L. Heilbron
THE HISTORY OF POLITICAL THOUGHT Richard Whatmore
THE HISTORY OF TIME Leofranc Holford-Strevens
HIV AND AIDS Alan Whiteside
HOBBES Richard Tuck
HOLLYWOOD Peter Decherney
THE HOLY ROMAN EMPIRE Joachim Whaley
HOME Michael Allen Fox
HOMER Barbara Graziosi
HORMONES Martin Luck
HORROR Darryl Jones
HUMAN ANATOMY Leslie Klenerman
HUMAN EVOLUTION Bernard Wood
HUMAN PHYSIOLOGY Jamie A. Davies
HUMAN RESOURCE MANAGEMENT Adrian Wilkinson
HUMAN RIGHTS Andrew Clapham
HUMANISM Stephen Law
HUME James A. Harris
HUMOUR Noël Carroll
IBN SĪNĀ (AVICENNA) Peter Adamson
THE ICE AGE Jamie Woodward
IDENTITY Florian Coulmas
IDEOLOGY Michael Freeden
IMAGINATION Jennifer Gosetti-Ferencei
THE IMMUNE SYSTEM Paul Klenerman
INDIAN CINEMA Ashish Rajadhyaksha
INDIAN PHILOSOPHY Sue Hamilton
THE INDUSTRIAL REVOLUTION Robert C. Allen
INFECTIOUS DISEASE Marta L. Wayne and Benjamin M. Bolker
INFINITY Ian Stewart
INFORMATION Luciano Floridi
INNOVATION Mark Dodgson and David Gann
INTELLECTUAL PROPERTY Siva Vaidhyanathan
INTELLIGENCE Ian J. Deary
INTERNATIONAL LAW Vaughan Lowe
INTERNATIONAL MIGRATION Khalid Koser
INTERNATIONAL RELATIONS Christian Reus-Smit
INTERNATIONAL SECURITY Christopher S. Browning
INSECTS Simon Leather
INVASIVE SPECIES Julie Lockwood and Dustin Welbourne
IRAN Ali M. Ansari
ISLAM Malise Ruthven
ISLAMIC HISTORY Adam Silverstein
ISLAMIC LAW Mashood A. Baderin
ISOTOPES Rob Ellam
ITALIAN LITERATURE Peter Hainsworth and David Robey
HENRY JAMES Susan L. Mizruchi
JAPANESE LITERATURE Alan Tansman
JESUS Richard Bauckham
JEWISH HISTORY David N. Myers
JEWISH LITERATURE Ilan Stavans
JOURNALISM Ian Hargreaves
JAMES JOYCE Colin MacCabe
JUDAISM Norman Solomon
JUNG Anthony Stevens
THE JURY Renée Lettow Lerner
KABBALAH Joseph Dan
KAFKA Ritchie Robertson
KANT Roger Scruton
KEYNES Robert Skidelsky
KIERKEGAARD Patrick Gardiner
KNOWLEDGE Jennifer Nagel
THE KORAN Michael Cook
KOREA Michael J. Seth
LAKES Warwick F. Vincent
LANDSCAPE ARCHITECTURE Ian H. Thompson
LANDSCAPES AND GEOMORPHOLOGY Andrew Goudie and Heather Viles
LANGUAGES Stephen R. Anderson
LATE ANTIQUITY Gillian Clark
LAW Raymond Wacks
THE LAWS OF THERMODYNAMICS Peter Atkins
LEADERSHIP Keith Grint
LEARNING Mark Haselgrove
LEIBNIZ Maria Rosa Antognazza
C. S. LEWIS James Como
LIBERALISM Michael Freeden

LIGHT Ian Walmsley
LINCOLN Allen C. Guelzo
LINGUISTICS Peter Matthews
LITERARY THEORY Jonathan Culler
LOCKE John Dunn
LOGIC Graham Priest
LOVE Ronald de Sousa
MARTIN LUTHER Scott H. Hendrix
MACHIAVELLI Quentin Skinner
MADNESS Andrew Scull
MAGIC Owen Davies
MAGNA CARTA Nicholas Vincent
MAGNETISM Stephen Blundell
MALTHUS Donald Winch
MAMMALS T. S. Kemp
MANAGEMENT John Hendry
NELSON MANDELA Elleke Boehmer
MAO Delia Davin
MARINE BIOLOGY Philip V. Mladenov
MARKETING Kenneth Le Meunier-FitzHugh
THE MARQUIS DE SADE John Phillips
MARTYRDOM Jolyon Mitchell
MARX Peter Singer
MATERIALS Christopher Hall
MATHEMATICAL ANALYSIS Richard Earl
MATHEMATICAL FINANCE Mark H. A. Davis
MATHEMATICS Timothy Gowers
MATTER Geoff Cottrell
THE MAYA Matthew Restall and Amara Solari
THE MEANING OF LIFE Terry Eagleton
MEASUREMENT David Hand
MEDICAL ETHICS Michael Dunn and Tony Hope
MEDICAL LAW Charles Foster
MEDIEVAL BRITAIN John Gillingham and Ralph A. Griffiths
MEDIEVAL LITERATURE Elaine Treharne
MEDIEVAL PHILOSOPHY John Marenbon
MEMORY Jonathan K. Foster
METAPHYSICS Stephen Mumford
METHODISM William J. Abraham
THE MEXICAN REVOLUTION Alan Knight
MICROBIOLOGY Nicholas P. Money
MICROBIOMES Angela E. Douglas
MICROECONOMICS Avinash Dixit
MICROSCOPY Terence Allen
THE MIDDLE AGES Miri Rubin
MILITARY JUSTICE Eugene R. Fidell
MILITARY STRATEGY Antulio J. Echevarria II
JOHN STUART MILL Gregory Claeys
MINERALS David Vaughan
MIRACLES Yujin Nagasawa
MODERN ARCHITECTURE Adam Sharr
MODERN ART David Cottington
MODERN BRAZIL Anthony W. Pereira
MODERN CHINA Rana Mitter
MODERN DRAMA Kirsten E. Shepherd-Barr
MODERN FRANCE Vanessa R. Schwartz
MODERN INDIA Craig Jeffrey
MODERN IRELAND Senia Pašeta
MODERN ITALY Anna Cento Bull
MODERN JAPAN Christopher Goto-Jones
MODERN LATIN AMERICAN LITERATURE Roberto González Echevarría
MODERN WAR Richard English
MODERNISM Christopher Butler
MOLECULAR BIOLOGY Aysha Divan and Janice A. Royds
MOLECULES Philip Ball
MONASTICISM Stephen J. Davis
THE MONGOLS Morris Rossabi
MONTAIGNE William M. Hamlin
MOONS David A. Rothery
MORMONISM Richard Lyman Bushman
MOUNTAINS Martin F. Price
MUHAMMAD Jonathan A. C. Brown
MULTICULTURALISM Ali Rattansi
MULTILINGUALISM John C. Maher
MUSIC Nicholas Cook
MUSIC AND TECHNOLOGY Mark Katz
MYTH Robert A. Segal
NANOTECHNOLOGY Philip Moriarty
NAPOLEON David A. Bell

THE NAPOLEONIC WARS
Mike Rapport
NATIONALISM Steven Grosby
NATIVE AMERICAN LITERATURE
Sean Teuton
NAVIGATION Jim Bennett
NAZI GERMANY Jane Caplan
NEGOTIATION Carrie Menkel-Meadow
NEOLIBERALISM Manfred B. Steger and Ravi K. Roy
NETWORKS Guido Caldarelli and Michele Catanzaro
THE NEW TESTAMENT
Luke Timothy Johnson
THE NEW TESTAMENT AS LITERATURE
Kyle Keefer
NEWTON Robert Iliffe
NIETZSCHE Michael Tanner
NINETEENTH-CENTURY BRITAIN
Christopher Harvie and H. C. G. Matthew
THE NORMAN CONQUEST
George Garnett
NORTH AMERICAN INDIANS
Theda Perdue and Michael D. Green
NORTHERN IRELAND
Marc Mulholland
NOTHING Frank Close
NUCLEAR PHYSICS Frank Close
NUCLEAR POWER Maxwell Irvine
NUCLEAR WEAPONS
Joseph M. Siracusa
NUMBER THEORY Robin Wilson
NUMBERS Peter M. Higgins
NUTRITION David A. Bender
OBJECTIVITY Stephen Gaukroger
OBSERVATIONAL ASTRONOMY
Geoff Cottrell
OCEANS Dorrik Stow
THE OLD TESTAMENT
Michael D. Coogan
THE ORCHESTRA D. Kern Holoman
ORGANIC CHEMISTRY
Graham Patrick
ORGANIZATIONS
Mary Jo Hatch
ORGANIZED CRIME
Georgios A. Antonopoulos and Georgios Papanicolaou
ORTHODOX CHRISTIANITY
A. Edward Siecienski
OVID Llewelyn Morgan
PAGANISM Owen Davies
PAKISTAN Pippa Virdee
THE PALESTINIAN-ISRAELI CONFLICT Martin Bunton
PANDEMICS Christian W. McMillen
PARTICLE PHYSICS Frank Close
PAUL E. P. Sanders
IVAN PAVLOV Daniel P. Todes
PEACE Oliver P. Richmond
PENTECOSTALISM William K. Kay
PERCEPTION Brian Rogers
THE PERIODIC TABLE Eric R. Scerri
PHILOSOPHICAL METHOD
Timothy Williamson
PHILOSOPHY Edward Craig
PHILOSOPHY IN THE ISLAMIC WORLD Peter Adamson
PHILOSOPHY OF BIOLOGY
Samir Okasha
PHILOSOPHY OF LAW
Raymond Wacks
PHILOSOPHY OF MIND
Barbara Gail Montero
PHILOSOPHY OF PHYSICS
David Wallace
PHILOSOPHY OF SCIENCE
Samir Okasha
PHILOSOPHY OF RELIGION
Tim Bayne
PHOTOGRAPHY Steve Edwards
PHYSICAL CHEMISTRY Peter Atkins
PHYSICS Sidney Perkowitz
PILGRIMAGE Ian Reader
PLAGUE Paul Slack
PLANETARY SYSTEMS
Raymond T. Pierrehumbert
PLANETS David A. Rothery
PLANTS Timothy Walker
PLATE TECTONICS Peter Molnar
PLATO Julia Annas
POETRY Bernard O'Donoghue
POLITICAL PHILOSOPHY
David Miller
POLITICS Kenneth Minogue
POLYGAMY Sarah M. S. Pearsall
POPULISM Cas Mudde and Cristóbal Rovira Kaltwasser

POSTCOLONIALISM
Robert J. C. Young
POSTMODERNISM Christopher Butler
POSTSTRUCTURALISM
Catherine Belsey
POVERTY Philip N. Jefferson
PREHISTORY Chris Gosden
PRESOCRATIC PHILOSOPHY
Catherine Osborne
PRIVACY Raymond Wacks
PROBABILITY John Haigh
PROGRESSIVISM Walter Nugent
PROHIBITION W. J. Rorabaugh
PROJECTS Andrew Davies
PROTESTANTISM Mark A. Noll
PSEUDOSCIENCE Michael D. Gordin
PSYCHIATRY Tom Burns
PSYCHOANALYSIS Daniel Pick
PSYCHOLOGY Gillian Butler and
Freda McManus
PSYCHOLOGY OF MUSIC
Elizabeth Hellmuth Margulis
PSYCHOPATHY Essi Viding
PSYCHOTHERAPY Tom Burns and
Eva Burns-Lundgren
PUBLIC ADMINISTRATION
Stella Z. Theodoulou and Ravi K. Roy
PUBLIC HEALTH Virginia Berridge
PURITANISM Francis J. Bremer
THE QUAKERS Pink Dandelion
QUANTUM THEORY
John Polkinghorne
RACISM Ali Rattansi
RADIOACTIVITY Claudio Tuniz
RASTAFARI Ennis B. Edmonds
READING Belinda Jack
THE REAGAN REVOLUTION Gil Troy
REALITY Jan Westerhoff
RECONSTRUCTION Allen C. Guelzo
THE REFORMATION Peter Marshall
REFUGEES Gil Loescher
RELATIVITY Russell Stannard
RELIGION Thomas A. Tweed
RELIGION IN AMERICA Timothy Beal
THE RENAISSANCE Jerry Brotton
RENAISSANCE ART
Geraldine A. Johnson
RENEWABLE ENERGY Nick Jelley
REPTILES T. S. Kemp
REVOLUTIONS Jack A. Goldstone
RHETORIC Richard Toye
RISK Baruch Fischhoff and John Kadvany
RITUAL Barry Stephenson
RIVERS Nick Middleton
ROBOTICS Alan Winfield
ROCKS Jan Zalasiewicz
ROMAN BRITAIN Peter Salway
THE ROMAN EMPIRE
Christopher Kelly
THE ROMAN REPUBLIC
David M. Gwynn
ROMANTICISM Michael Ferber
ROUSSEAU Robert Wokler
RUSSELL A. C. Grayling
THE RUSSIAN ECONOMY
Richard Connolly
RUSSIAN HISTORY Geoffrey Hosking
RUSSIAN LITERATURE Catriona Kelly
THE RUSSIAN REVOLUTION
S. A. Smith
SAINTS Simon Yarrow
SAMURAI Michael Wert
SAVANNAS Peter A. Furley
SCEPTICISM Duncan Pritchard
SCHIZOPHRENIA Chris Frith and
Eve Johnstone
SCHOPENHAUER
Christopher Janaway
SCIENCE AND RELIGION
Thomas Dixon and Adam R. Shapiro
SCIENCE FICTION David Seed
THE SCIENTIFIC REVOLUTION
Lawrence M. Principe
SCOTLAND Rab Houston
SECULARISM Andrew Copson
SEXUAL SELECTION Marlene Zuk and
Leigh W. Simmons
SEXUALITY Véronique Mottier
WILLIAM SHAKESPEARE
Stanley Wells
SHAKESPEARE'S COMEDIES
Bart van Es
SHAKESPEARE'S SONNETS AND
POEMS Jonathan F. S. Post
SHAKESPEARE'S TRAGEDIES
Stanley Wells
GEORGE BERNARD SHAW
Christopher Wixson
MARY SHELLEY Charlotte Gordon
THE SHORT STORY Andrew Kahn

SIKHISM Eleanor Nesbitt
SILENT FILM Donna Kornhaber
THE SILK ROAD James A. Millward
SLANG Jonathon Green
SLEEP Steven W. Lockley and Russell G. Foster
SMELL Matthew Cobb
ADAM SMITH Christopher J. Berry
SOCIAL AND CULTURAL ANTHROPOLOGY John Monaghan and Peter Just
SOCIAL PSYCHOLOGY Richard J. Crisp
SOCIAL WORK Sally Holland and Jonathan Scourfield
SOCIALISM Michael Newman
SOCIOLINGUISTICS John Edwards
SOCIOLOGY Steve Bruce
SOCRATES C. C. W. Taylor
SOFT MATTER Tom McLeish
SOUND Mike Goldsmith
SOUTHEAST ASIA James R. Rush
THE SOVIET UNION Stephen Lovell
THE SPANISH CIVIL WAR Helen Graham
SPANISH LITERATURE Jo Labanyi
THE SPARTANS Andrew J. Bayliss
SPINOZA Roger Scruton
SPIRITUALITY Philip Sheldrake
SPORT Mike Cronin
STARS Andrew King
STATISTICS David J. Hand
STEM CELLS Jonathan Slack
STOICISM Brad Inwood
STRUCTURAL ENGINEERING David Blockley
STUART BRITAIN John Morrill
SUBURBS Carl Abbott
THE SUN Philip Judge
SUPERCONDUCTIVITY Stephen Blundell
SUPERSTITION Stuart Vyse
SYMMETRY Ian Stewart
SYNAESTHESIA Julia Simner
SYNTHETIC BIOLOGY Jamie A. Davies
SYSTEMS BIOLOGY Eberhard O. Voit
TAXATION Stephen Smith
TEETH Peter S. Ungar
TERRORISM Charles Townshend
THEATRE Marvin Carlson
THEOLOGY David F. Ford
THINKING AND REASONING Jonathan St B. T. Evans
THOUGHT Tim Bayne
TIBETAN BUDDHISM Matthew T. Kapstein
TIDES David George Bowers and Emyr Martyn Roberts
TIME Jenann Ismael
TOCQUEVILLE Harvey C. Mansfield
LEO TOLSTOY Liza Knapp
TOPOLOGY Richard Earl
TRAGEDY Adrian Poole
TRANSLATION Matthew Reynolds
THE TREATY OF VERSAILLES Michael S. Neiberg
TRIGONOMETRY Glen Van Brummelen
THE TROJAN WAR Eric H. Cline
TRUST Katherine Hawley
THE TUDORS John Guy
TWENTIETH-CENTURY BRITAIN Kenneth O. Morgan
TYPOGRAPHY Paul Luna
THE UNITED NATIONS Jussi M. Hanhimäki
UNIVERSITIES AND COLLEGES David Palfreyman and Paul Temple
THE U.S. CIVIL WAR Louis P. Masur
THE U.S. CONGRESS Donald A. Ritchie
THE U.S. CONSTITUTION David J. Bodenhamer
THE U.S. SUPREME COURT Linda Greenhouse
UTILITARIANISM Katarzyna de Lazari-Radek and Peter Singer
UTOPIANISM Lyman Tower Sargent
VATICAN II Shaun Blanchard and Stephen Bullivant
VETERINARY SCIENCE James Yeates
THE VICTORIANS Martin Hewitt
THE VIKINGS Julian D. Richards
VIOLENCE Philip Dwyer
THE VIRGIN MARY Mary Joan Winn Leith
THE VIRTUES Craig A. Boyd and Kevin Timpe
VIRUSES Dorothy H. Crawford
VOLCANOES Michael J. Branney and Jan Zalasiewicz

VOLTAIRE Nicholas Cronk
WAR AND RELIGION
Jolyon Mitchell and Joshua Rey
WAR AND TECHNOLOGY
Alex Roland
WATER John Finney
WAVES Mike Goldsmith
WEATHER Storm Dunlop
THE WELFARE STATE David Garland
WITCHCRAFT Malcolm Gaskill
WITTGENSTEIN A. C. Grayling
WORK Stephen Fineman
WORLD MUSIC Philip Bohlman
WORLD MYTHOLOGY David Leeming
THE WORLD TRADE ORGANIZATION
Amrita Narlikar
WORLD WAR II Gerhard L. Weinberg
WRITING AND SCRIPT
Andrew Robinson
ZIONISM Michael Stanislawski
ÉMILE ZOLA Brian Nelson

Available soon:

CIVIL WARS Monica Duffy Toft
THE GULAG Alan Barenberg

For more information visit our website

www.oup.com/vsi/

Jennifer Gosetti-Ferencei

IMAGINATION

A Very Short Introduction

OXFORD
UNIVERSITY PRESS

OXFORD
UNIVERSITY PRESS

Great Clarendon Street, Oxford, OX2 6DP,
United Kingdom

Oxford University Press is a department of the University of Oxford.
It furthers the University's objective of excellence in research, scholarship,
and education by publishing worldwide. Oxford is a registered trade mark of
Oxford University Press in the UK and in certain other countries

© Jennifer Gosetti-Ferencei 2023

The moral rights of the author have been asserted

All rights reserved. No part of this publication may be reproduced, stored in
a retrieval system, or transmitted, in any form or by any means, without the
prior permission in writing of Oxford University Press, or as expressly permitted
by law, by licence or under terms agreed with the appropriate reprographics
rights organization. Enquiries concerning reproduction outside the scope of the
above should be sent to the Rights Department, Oxford University Press, at the
address above

You must not circulate this work in any other form
and you must impose this same condition on any acquirer

Published in the United States of America by Oxford University Press
198 Madison Avenue, New York, NY 10016, United States of America

British Library Cataloguing in Publication Data
Data available

Library of Congress Control Number: 2023936565

ISBN 978–0–19–883002–3

Printed and bound by
CPI Group (UK) Ltd, Croydon, CR0 4YY

Links to third party websites are provided by Oxford in good faith and
for information only. Oxford disclaims any responsibility for the materials
contained in any third party website referenced in this work.

MIX
Paper | Supporting
responsible forestry
FSC
www.fsc.org
FSC® C013604